PLURALISTIC SOCIETY, PLURALISTIC CHURCH

Benjamin R. Mariante

UNIVERSITY
PRESS OF
AMERICA

Library of Congress Catalog Card Number: **80-69058**

ACKNOWLEDGEMENTS

No book is the product of one person's efforts,
and this one as much as any has benefited from the
time, energy and intelligence of many people. First
to be remembered and acknowledged is the late
Arthur C. McGill of Harvard Divinity School.
Art enriched the lives of all of us who came in
contact with him, and his help and encouragement
provided me with sustenance at some dark moments.
Two other persons at Harvard Divinity School
demonstrated faith in this project, J. Lawrence
Burkholder, now president of Goshen College and
Harvey Cox, whose ebullience infects us all.

Two sociologists were of immense help in suggesting
and supporting this idea, Rev. Eugene Schallert, S.J.,
of Loyola University, Los Angeles, and Donald P.
Warwick of Harvard. Both encouraged and supported
ideas of mine and helped me to bake fully some half-
baked ones.

Several people provided editorial and typing help,
chief of whom is our dear friend, Rose Mary Kirwin,
as well as Elsie Simmons and Margaret Peters.
They deserve a debt of gratitude for their struggles
with my arcane syntax. I would like as well to
thank Robert Kruse, C.S.C., Academic Dean of Stonehill
College, for encouragement and generous support.

Finally it is a tradition for authors to thank
their families and this author is not about to break
with tradition. Ann provided more than enough support
through many a slough of despondency and Jonathan
provided enough distraction to prevent me from taking
myself too seriously. In many ways the book is
really his for to him belongs the transcendent
future.

Easton, Massachusetts
June 1, 1981

TABLE OF CONTENTS

PART I

BIBLICAL PREPARATION

CHAPTER I

PART II

SOCIOLOGICAL ANALYSIS

CHAPTER 2

PART III

THEOLOGICAL APPLICATION

CHAPTER 4

A theology that proceeds
in a step-by-step correlation
with what can be said about
man empirically is well
worth a serious try.

--- Peter Berger

INTRODUCTION

A hundred years ago, or perhaps a hundred
and fifty years ago, the family of a coal miner in
Wales might be seated around a dinner table and
their lives would be plotted for them. It was
possible to predict, at least statistically, where
all of them would be located on the total social
scale five, ten, thirty years hence. Their
occupations, religion, income, value system,
geographical location, political views and life-
span were laid out before them. There was neither
altering nor questioning.

Today all would be different. The coal
miner's family, watching television, would in
fact see each member's life as opening up into
uncharted territory. The unexpected, the unpre-
dicted could in fact happen to any of them. It
had happened to others; and their sons, nephews,
young husbands could become famous pop-singers,
like Tom Jones, or actors trained in the classical
tradition, like Richard Burton.[1] Life has moved
from total predictability to radical uncertainty;
and this radical uncertainty is viewed not only
as entirely acceptable but as at least better
than anything that has preceded it in the social
order.

How do we explain this change that has
occured in the course of the past century?
The answer to that is far too complex for any
one book or for a single investigation; but one
aspect of this change that hasn't been fully explored is "pluralization", the co-existence
of many worlds of values and of opportunities.
This is the new institutional patterning that
has developed in our society; and it is the
effects of this patterning, specifically on religious institutions, churches, that we will
examine here.

The focus of this work is not primarily to examine religious institutions as social institutions, although this aspect of churches or the Church cannot be ignored. Rather I wish to look at religious institutions as religious, and so this work is primarily a theological essay. Nevertheless it is not possible to ignore the sociological aspects of pluralization; and in fact, as a work in Applied Theology it is directed toward making an explicit and direct relationship between sociology and theology.

PLAN OF THE INVESTIGATION

After a brief chapter on the Scriptural foundations for pluriformity in the Church, the first part of this monograph, consisting of two chapters, is concerned with a sociological analysis, specifically with the sociology of pluralism. None of the work in these two chapters represents original research in the sociological understanding of research. It is an attempt to assemble and collate data from various sources, primary, such as government documents and reports, and secondary, from the research of others, to establish the fact of pluralism in some systematic way and to present an analysis of this modern social phenomenon with specific reference to its impact on religious institutions.

The last three chapters, the second part of this monograph, deal with the Church, especially with ecclesiology, the theology of the Church, in light of this modern social situation, socio-cultural pluralism. Not only Church forms and Church structures are affected by and respond to the social situation; theology as well is deepened, altered or re-arranged as it confronts new or different environments. This change or development in theology and its application are the central concern of this work.

Pierre Babin has remarked in this regard that at present "the major influence on ... the Church

xii

seems to be the cultural change currently trans-
forming various structures of thinking, seeing
and learning ... The transition to a pluralistic
society demands new ways of learning and new
requirements for the proposition of faith."[2]
And for the most, this transition also demands a
re-examination of the possibilities of the Church.
As Pierre Babin notes, is it possible "to live
as Christians without belonging to a caste"?[3]

It is necessary to look at what has occurred
in the transition which our society has undergone,
to examine empirically the new socio-cultural
milieu in which the Church is now located.

Superficially the fragmentation of society
has brought about an apparent disintegration
of the value structure. The overarching,
legitimating "sacred cosmos" seems to have broken
down. However, we must look more closely at the
situation. Apparent fragmentation is perhaps
only specialization and each specialty in society
may have developed its own value structure and
internal legitimation.

In this work, then, I have chosen to concentrate on an analysis of "secondary institutions"
in society, particularly the economy and the polity,
because these secondary institutions have assumed
such a prominent, some would say, dominant position
in our society. But this analysis and its impact
on ecclesiology and Church structure is not
restricted to the area of secondary institutions.
The ecclesiology of a multiform Church can be
applied to other instances in similar cultural
situations. Examples of this might occur in the
case of international cultural pluralism. The
Indian Liturgical Conference is attempting to
formulate a liturgical style based on Indian
cultural themes that can be incorporated into
and made part of an "Indian theology".[4] A
second example of a different application of the
theology developed here would be in the situation
of ethnic pluralism. If, as seems evident from

xiii

the statistical analyses, the United States
(and other countries, such as Canada and Australia)
is a nation of minorities, then a pluriform
Church would seem appropriate in such a cultural
situation.

AN "INTENTIONAL ECCLESIOLOGY"

However, I believe that the importance of
this view of ecclesiology stems not from its
specific applications but from the new possibilities
that have come about because of breakthroughs
in the social sciences, not the least of which is
a sense of history and the possibility of
creating our own destiny.

Cliché though this may be, the
development of predictive models of
total social structures has gone
sufficiently far to point up the fact
that total social breakdown can only
be avoided by radical decisions on
the type of society and the type of man
that we wish to create.[5]

Thus it lies within our power to create the kind
of society we want. No one doubts the serious-
ness of this task; and the believer must be
convinced that "the Church" must somehow be
present at the creation. The Church cannot be
on the sidelines; and yet the Church cannot control society or its development. The Church is
presence, witness, "sign", not in some passive
way, but actively, engaged, dedicated. The
implication of all this is that the Church herself
must be self-conscious, must be born anew,
reformanda, for this as for every age. The
Church is reflective witness, reflective on its
own constitution; it is intentional, those who
are its members decide on their commitment to
Church and world; it is a self-conscious sign,
actively present in the world to direct the world
toward its own destiny and fulfillment. The new
possibility for society calls forth a renewed

xiv

vision of the Church.

Thus the hypothetical family of a century ago was not an example chosen arbitrarily. It is an example that fits our impressions and the facts that are available. It is true that our society presents new possibilities, even if this seems a tired and trite slogan. But we know that the "occupational status of the average man in contemporary industrial societies is much less affected by that of his father than it was in earlier societies."[6] Kahan in one of the most thorough studies of this sort, of Russian workers, found that "the supply of hereditary workers exceeded the rate of increase of the total labor force"[7] in the last half of the nineteenth century. Kahan's material shows a high proportion of hereditary workers. Then the individual's life and life-style were truly predictable.

Now all this has changed, and the Church also has changed. The question isn't whether the Church will change or must change in confronting a radically different social reality. Of course, the Church changes (and in certain fundamental ways remains the same). Our present knowledge now allows for directed change, not only of "secular" social institutions, but of the religious institutions we are familiar with, the Church. It is the possibility of an "intentional Church", a directed and self-reflective ecclesial community that can meet the changing world that is the issue here. For the Church herself must consider what she wants to be and to do in a new and challenging social order.

REFERENCES

1. I am indebted to Arthur C. McGill for this homely example of an imaginative introduction to the most complex topic "pluralism".

2. Babin, Pierre, <u>Adolescents</u> <u>in</u> <u>Search</u> <u>of</u> <u>a</u> <u>New</u> <u>Church</u>. New York: Herder & Herder, 1969. p. 23.

3. <u>Ibid</u>., p. 21.

4. This information comes from personal conversation with Rev. Gerwin van Leeuwen, O.F.M., who is one of the theological consultants to the Indian Liturgical Conference. He works at the Ecumenical Institute in Bangalore.

5. Elliott, Charles, "An Esoteric Critique of Cartigny", in <u>In</u> <u>Search</u> <u>of</u> <u>a</u> <u>Theology</u> <u>of</u> <u>Development</u>. Papers from a Consultation on Theology and Development held by Sodepax in Cartigny, Switzerland, November, 1969. Geneva: Committee on Society, Development and Peace, 1969. pp. 16-17.

6. Caplow, Theodore, <u>Elementary</u> <u>Sociology</u>. Englewood Cliffs: Prentice Hall, 1971. p. 392.

7. Kahan, Arcadius, "The "Hereditary Worker" Hypothesis and the Development of a Factory Labor Force in Eighteenth- and Nineteenth-Century Russia", in Anderson, C. Arnold and Broman, Mary Jean, (eds.) <u>Education</u> <u>and</u> <u>Economic</u> <u>Development</u>. Chicago: Aldine, 1965. p. 295.

PART I.

BIBLICAL PREPARATION.

CHAPTER I

NEW TESTAMENT CHURCHES

It is generally true that Christian theology seeks to justify itself by establishing some relationship to the New Testament. This desire to seek New Testament justification for doctrinal statements is not a false or whimsical task, for Christianity as a religion must seek its contacts with that originating and orienting experience from which the totality of Christian life has flowered for twenty centuries.

Yet there is some danger in this "quest for origins". First, as has been critically indicated more than once, such a quest may in fact lead to an archaic and arcane "primitivism" which, rather than orienting a flourishing religious experience, mummifies and crystalizes religious forms and so prevents the flowering of religion as envisaged by the original religious genius or charismatic founder and those who shared this original experience. Such a primitivism would arrest Christianity at the time of Jesus or of the Apostolic Church.

Secondly and deriving from this, there is the danger that a search for original authenticity may blind the seekers to authentic development, especially with regard to such a rich and articulated religion as Christianity.[1] Authentic development in Christianity has taken two basic forms and both seem to apply to Christian theology and to that area of Christian doctrine that is called ecclesiology, the theology of the Church.

One kind of development consists in unfolding and realizing the full implications that are in the original "revelation" or religious tradition. The metaphor often used in this regard is that of "the acorn and the oak". In potentia, everything is already present in the acorn; the proper circumstances are all that are needed to bring about the full development of the oak tree. The proper social, cultural, historical or even spiritual circumstances can bring about the religious flowering of the tradition, the revelation. This notion of development in theology is usually called "continuity" or "continuous doctrinal development".[2]

It is possible that development or change can come about in another way. A new element can be introduced into the tradition from outside the tradition, from the ambience, the social order, another religious tradition, or in a variety of ways. This new element is then assimilated and integrated into the tradition and gradually becomes a part of the accepted and authentic complex that is regarded as the orienting and originating religious experience. This idea of development is usually designated by the term "discontinuity", or "discontinuous development".[3]

In this chapter, I don't intend to make any judgments about the kind of development that occurred in New Testament ecclesiology, although I believe that a case can be made for the second or discontinuous development of ecclesiology. Rather I wish to indicate that in the New Testament period already a plurality of both ecclesial forms and ecclesiologies existed and that as a consequences we need have no hesitancy today about accepting a pluriform Church in our contemporary social order.

At the same time, I am aware of the caveats indicated at the outset, namely, primitivism and blindness to authentic development; and I am not opting for a simple return to either earlier Church forms or ecclesiologies. Indeed as I hope to make clear in the second part of this monograph, our ecclesiological understanding today is much more "sophisticated", and hopefully even better capable of dealing with a multi-form church. The principle effort in this chapter is simply to show that the

New Testament gives indications of the possibility
of a plurality of church structures and a pluralistic ecclesiology.

.· In this connection it is important to note
Käsemann's caution: "The New Testament does not
present us with an ecclesiologia perennis but
offers us instead certain ecclesiological archetypes."[4]
There are two statements here. First we are warned
not to search for some absolute ecclesiological
norm, an ecclesiologia perennis, in the New
Testament, and by implication in the early Church
as a whole. Rather, and this is the second point,
we have archetypes, more than one model or form,
which not only are to provide the bases for future
models, but also present an archetypal situation
of plurality. It does not seem inconceivable,
than, in terms of New Testament evidence that
certain models or forms might exist today and
need conscious explication or theological interpretation.

DIFFERENT CHURCH STYLES IN DIFFERENT LOCATIONS

According to many New Testament scholars,
it seems that there were different Church forms
in the different centers when the early Church
began to gain a sufficiently large number of
converts. As Schmidt points out in his famous
article: "It is quite possible, and wholly natural,
that many matters of organization in Christian
congregations should have been regulated according
to the pattern of contemporary societies."[5]
Schmidt, however, was not concerned to follow
this up as a theological statement; he was referring
principally to the political and social organization
in the Hellenistic world into which the Church
moved in a very short time.

Contemporary exegetes, however, do regard
this as an area for theological investigation and
believe that these matters of organization reflected
distinct ecclesiologies and quite different styles
of theologizing as well. Schnackenburg describes

3

three different "living communities" as reflective
of different ways of "being the Church".[6]

In Jerusalem, we can discern a particular trend
in the Christian community. There is a strong
dependence on "apostolic" leadership (Acts 2:42; 5:12)
even Paul seeks some kind of confirmation from this
leadership. (Gal. 1:18; 2:2). There is a rich
liturgial life, based partly on temple worship
and partly on what seems to have been Eucharistic
celebration in the houses of members of the congregation. (Acts 5:12b and 3:11. Both aspects
of liturgical life are joined seemingly in 2:46
and 5:42.) This seems to indicate, as well a
sense of strong continuity with Israel and positive
attachment to and regard for the Temple. The
Jerusalem Church also stressed the community
holding of goods in some way, whether obligatory or
voluntary is of some dispute. Whatever the Lucan
embellishments (as well as the softenings of
conflict) of this picture, it seems that a definite
ecclesiology emerges from the Jerusalem Church,
stressing "apostolic and hierarchical" leadership,
continuity with Jewish worship and ritual, and
communal sharing in some way of material goods.

At Antioch, a mixed community of Jews and pagans
(Acts 11:19-21), we witness what is apparently a
somewhat different development. Their reliance
for leadership seemed to be placed on "charismatic
gifts", so that "prophets and teachers" (Acts 13:1;
cf. also 11:27) assume a somewhat central position.
This emphasis on charismatic gifts may reflect
the tradition of the missionizing of Antioch that
is reported in Acts 11:21: "The power of the Lord
was with them, and a great many became believers,
and turned to the Lord." (NEB) We find also an
emphasis on instruction (Acts 11:26) and also on
unity within and among congregations.

Finally the Corinthian Church provides us with
an example of a third kind of development. Here
is a Church predominantly of pagan origin. We
find here, according to the descriptions from

Paul's two letters, not only a rich charismatic
endowment but special emphasis on charismatic
life in the Church. This emphasis has, sadly, led
to confusion and even division (1 Cor. 14), and
division existed even at the Lord's Supper cele-
brations. Yet it was also this ritual life, of
baptism and eucharist, which provided a rich and
shared religious experience that seems to stand
at the core of the community and provides much of
its basis as a Church (e.g., 1 Cor. 10:16-17).
At the same time, the Church is clearly distinguished - and this appears to be a matter of some
import - not only from the pagans but even from
the Jews (1 Cor. 10:18-22, 32. Cf. 2 Cor. 6:14 -
7:1).

Thus these examples present us with three
quite different pictures of Church life and yet
no one would deny that any of them was less
"faithful" to the Lord of the Church. Indeed,
Paul encouraged the great collection among the
Corinthians, pagan converts, as a bond of unity
to brother and sister Christians in the Jerusalem
Church of Jewish Christians. Yet it seems from
the evidence at hand that when we get to the
basic layer of Christian Church life we have in
these three instances different polities, ecclesiologies and theologies.

One further example should bring out this
difference in Church life that indeed suggests a
difference in ecclesiologies: the early conflict
in Jerusalem.

DOCTRINAL DIFFERENTIATION IN ONE LOCATION

Scriptural exegesis has reached a point, in
examination of the life of the early Church, where
it is possible to sort out various strands, traditions, and indeed, to see where the author has tried
to conciliate or smooth over conflicts and divisions
that existed in some of the earliest communities.
One such instance seems to be the divergencies

that developed in the early Christian community at Jerusalem. Contemporary exegesis leads us to the conclusion that there can be no doubt that a serious divergence on the nature of the Church developed in Jerusalem, although the Lucan account tries to smooth over some of the sharper contrasts.

One group in Jerusalem seemed to "hold fast" to many of the forms, structures and traditions of the Jewish theology of the time. Schweizer lists some of the elements that make up this ecclesiology: temple attendance, fidelity to the Sabbath, attention to food ordinances, and most basically, reliance on the authority both of the law and of the rabbinic tradition.[7] This is a concept of Church order and of ecclesiology that continued according to established Jewish forms.

The other group "declares its opposition to temple and law".[8] But these Hellenistic Jews in Jerusalem -- for this is what this group seems to have been -- seemed to go much further. Exegetes now are fairly certain that they proposed a concept of Church and Church order that differed in several fundamental ways from the basic ideas of the other, more "traditional" group. While maintaining that they too were relying on the teachings of the Old Testament, "Stephen, and other Hellenists of Jerusalem, emphasized those features of Jesus' teaching that pointed towards a 'radical reform that would break down the framework of legalism and ritualism.'"[9] This is a very different ecclesial view, indicative in fact of a tension that has remained in the Church until the present. Thus those differences that appeared in the early Jerusalem community are more than a matter of order or arrangment; they refer to a profound theological concept of Jesus' mission and of his commission to his followers.

A careful reading of Acts 4:32 - 8:1a reveals that theology is indeed a participant in the polity, order and form of the Church,[10] and is seen as such even in the sources that Luke (whatever the name of the "author" of _Acts_) used. In fact, Luke

6

indicates, or at least plainly leaves the evidence of ecclesial pluriformity in the same context in the first part of the text. As Raymond Brown points out:

> In ecclesiology, Luke in the Book of Acts makes no attempt to suppress the information that the Hellenist Christians objected to the type of organization prevalent among the Jewish Christians.
>
> Thus to ask us to believe that there was absolute uniformity of theology among the different groups or theologians represented in the New Testament is to ask us to deny obvious evidence. (Indeed, has there ever been absolute uniformity in any stage of Christianity?)[11]

We should now turn briefly to investigate these groups and theologians that we encounter in the New Testament.

DIFFERING NEW TESTAMENT ECCLESIOLOGIES

A brief survey of the various conceptions, forms and practices of the New Testament Church will be enough to show that diversity was one source of the vitality in the original and originating Church. It will also provide us with a new way to understand the multiform development in Christianity today. However, because this chapter is not concerned with developing a complete New Testament doctrinal ecclesiology, but with establishing a theological foundation, the method in the remainder of this chapter will be simple. Basically relying on the work of two recognized exegetes who differ considerably in their conceptions of the Church, but agree that there are different New Testament conceptions of the Church, I will present their conclusions about which there is substantial agreement in their discussion of

7

these differing conceptions. Mainly then I shall
rely on Eduard Schweizer's Church Order in the
New Testament and Rudolf Schnackenburg's The
Church in the New Testament.[12]

1. The Primitive Church as ecclesial community.[13]

     The early disciples apparently did not designate
themselves as a "holy remnant", a separate group
that was representative of God's design in some
way as a religious association. This seems to
have been the Qumran solution, but was foreign
to the primitive Church.[14] There was however a
sense of continuity with Israel. The primitive
Church settled in Jerusalem, was anxious to have
the complement of "Twelve", recalling the twelve
tribes, and like Jesus was conscious of a mission
to the "lost sheep of the house of Israel" (Matt.
15:24. Cf. Acts 2:36). Thus the "primitive
Church" in Jerusalem did not see itself as a
revolutionary group, breaking with Israel: continuity
was at the forefront of their ecclesiology.

     Yet a certain "looseness" begins to develop
about order and leadership. Certain traditional
regulations are no longer seen as essential, new
leaders (e.g., the "seven", prophets alongside
apostles, etc.) appear and there remains an openness in regard to the matter of settling the
question of the Gentiles. This does not mean that
these questions were settled, early, easily or
quickly; what Schweizer and Schnackenburg see
evidence of is a lack of rigidity in ecclesial life
already at this early stage.[15]

2. The Synoptic Gospels and the Church.

     Both Schweizer and Schnackenburg consider the
synoptic tradition of the Church before the Pauline,
although some Pauline writing undoubtedly precedes
both Matthew and Luke. (Both omit any systematic
consideration of Mark.) The Synoptic view of the
Church is regarded as transitional. Both Matthew

8

and Luke see the Church in continuity with Israel; and with neither is there the same kind of distinction that seems to develop in Pauline theology and the theology that derives from Paul.

a) The Lucan conception.[16]

A principle contribution of Luke's ecclesiology is to locate the Church in history. Luke insists on the ignorance of the date of God's final breakthrough into history (Luke 17:20-21 Acts 1:7); this ignorance establishes the relationship between the Church and history. The Church has its tasks for the present time, which is assuming a central focus in Church life and thought;[17] and the Church is to be the instrument of Christ in this historical epoch between the first and second coming of Jesus. Thus the Church and history are part of God's plan of salvation and the Church is to work in and through history to actualize this plan, but of course under the power and direction of the Spirit. Luke's Church is pneumatological, and because it is the same Spirit who directs history and the Church, the Church can remain open to any development. (Cf. Acts 16:9-10, crucial in this respect. Note the shift to a "we" passage.)

One further aspect of Luke's idea of the Church is important. Because this is a Church involved in history, it is inevitably involved in suffering. The Holy Spirit is consolation for the Church in this era of suffering, but adversity and trial are inevitable. Historical time is a time of tribulation and martyrdom; only when the Kingdom comes, will all that be behind the Church (Luke 21:36). Meanwhile, the Church must work through its relationship with history in the midst of trial, but always with the consolation of the Spirit of Jesus.

b) The Church in Matthew's Gospel.[18]

The Gospel of Matthew insists on the openness

and breadth of the universal community of the redeemed, a redeemed community not shut off against the Gentiles (Matt. 23:14). But there is a fundamental spiritual unity in this group, in spite of its breadth, a unity not based on blood and nationality, but in "attachment to the new teacher of the law."[19] For as the Church, in this view, is the fulfillment of Israel and regards itself as Israel, so it is a band of believers obedient to the "law". But this law is known, and especially is interpreted, only through Jesus, the Messiah and the Son of God. Thus the Church is conscious of obeying the law in a new way, found only through Jesus.

Yet this law, ever freshly interpreted, is normative for the Church and the standard of judgment[20]-- and of admittance, ultimately, to the Kingdom. For the Church in Matthew's view is subject to deficiency and even admits sinfulness, at least in its members. It is a mixed body, not like Luke's conception of Jews and Gentiles, but of good and bad. Even now the ekklesia can expel those who do not listen (Matt. 18:18); but ultimately it will be Jesus himself who determines admittance to the Kingdom (Matt. 25).

Nonetheless the Church has authority, conferred by Jesus, to establish order, "to bind and loose". This power to order itself, however, carries implications of service, humility and responsibility. Beyond this, such power is based on the certainty of the presence of the Lord. Through the power and manifestation of the Spirit of God, the Church is commissioned and assured of itself as the real Israel. The Church thus is to follow Jesus who is Spirit-filled (not the Church specifically) without hypocrisy, in lowliness, humility and meekness, even in willingness to sacrifice itself in following the Spirit empowered Lord.

The differences as well as similarities between the Lucan and Matthean ecclesiology and ecclesial structure are evident. While both start from the same notion of continuity with Israel, Luke's Church is pneumatological; Matthew de-emphasizes the pneuma, especially with regard to the Church, but insists on a "living law". It is this law that gives shape to the Church and provides the power of discrimination; Luke views the relationship between the Church and history as providing form and structure for the Church. Yet both see the Church as suffering, lowly, humble and even humiliated until the Lord comes again.

3. Paul's Theology of the Church.

Books and monographs have been written about Pauline ecclesiology and even about aspects of his doctrine of the Church.[21] Here my purpose is merely to give a sketch of the structure of his ecclesiology in order to see the developing pattern of diversity in New Testament ecclesiologies.

It is important to stress Paul's sense of discontinuity in continuity, a continuing paradox that runs through much of his writing. The Church is the true Israel because she is in fact the new Israel, at times, at least presented as sharply distinct from the old.[22] The genuineness of the new Israel depends on faith, itself the gift from and of God's freedom. This faith relied on the promises which are completed and totally fulfilled "in Christ Jesus". Those then who adhere to Christ in faith, who in fact and in faith constitute a body with Him constitute also the new Israel. So it is possible to apply every attribute of Israel to the Church insofar as it is "in Christ".

In contrast then to Matthew, the Church of God is not a mixtum compositum. There is no room for those who are not faithful, of the faith. The Church is the body of Christ, local, and in later theology, universal; and this presupposes that everyone who is a member of that body is saved. Certainly Paul affirms the sinfulness of all (cf. Rom. 3:22); but all of those who have received and accepted the gift of grace are saved. The Church in Paul's view is thus filled with the

11

Spirit of God's grace, and every individual believer is pneumatic.

However, in Paul's view of the Spirit and his work in the believing Church, he differs considerably from the Lucan doctrine. While for Luke the Spirit enables the Church and each member to fulfill his special historical mission, the Pauline view of the Spirit is the gift of the power of God "which gives faith and causes man to live in faith".[23] It is this radical action of the Spirit that breaks through history to freely elect the new, true Israel. The Spirit is not so much action in Church and world, as separating Church from the believing world. Paul thus affirms as primary the eschatological character of the Church, although he does not deny temporal and historical dimensions.

Paul's most creative insight into the mystery of the Church is generally regarded to be his notion of the Body of Christ. This is connected with his idea of the faithful, Spirit-gifted Church. This vision of the Church, a Body of Head and members, allows both for weakness and deficiency of the individual members at the same time as it affirms the essential unity and "grace-fullness" of the Church. This concept also allows in the Pauline (or Pauline inspired) letters to the Colossians and Ephesians the harmonizing of the polarities of eschatological and incarnational aspects not only of ecclesiology but of many areas of theology.

Thus, Paul's view of the Church, which in its earlier formulations at least, predates Matthew and Luke, differs in some significant ways from the synoptics; and in certain aspects seems more definitive than theirs. It would seem to provide a basis for ecclesial structures somewhat different from others we have seen.

4. <u>Ecclesiology in I Peter and in Hebrews.</u>[24]

While Schweizer warns us not to read too much
into I Peter, especially the famous ecclesiology of
the second chapter,25 nonetheless a definite
ecclesiology emerges from this brief writing, particularly when the whole epistle is analyzed with
reference to the celebrated section, 2:4-10. What
is of special interest for our purposes begins
with a consideration of the centrality of Christ
in this ecclesiology.

Christ is the living cornerstone around which
all else in the Church revolves, lives and grows.
He is the sociological and historical reference
point for the Christian community. Sociologically,26
it is He who can and does provide bonds of unity
for the Church; consequently, "Church" throughout
this epistle refers first of all to the universal
Church and only secondarily to the local Church.
Thus the "Flock of God" (5:2) is the Church in its
totality manifested in a special way in the local
congregation.

Historically the author sees a real break with
Judaism in its rejection of Christ; thus Christ
is the "cornerstone" of the historical process
that involves the Church's pilgrimage through
time. For the Church has an alien character in
the world; it is on pilgrimage in a foreign land.
And it is this notion of pilgrim Church that finds
its resonance in the pilgrim people idea recorded
in the Epistle to the Hebrews.

The organizing idea in the rather fully
developed ecclesiology of Hebrews is the vision
of a journeying people. It ties together the
principle ecclesiological themes: people of God,
pilgrimage, the future city, the heavenly
Jerusalem.27 This idea of a journey, a pilgrimage,
emphasizes the historicity of the Church, even
though it already has certain ties "in heaven".
Jesus has already inaugurated the last phase of
history and the Church has now to reach its goal.
Its beginning and end are in and with Christ,
its Leader. Thus the Church has a specific

eschatological direction, for those who follow this Leader are indeed the eschatological people of God.

However, union with Christ is not emphasized, as in I Peter and Paul. Rather Christ is seen as representative of the people, and his work and message establish a definitive and final covenant. One task of the Church is to protect and transmit this official "message" of the tradition from Jesus. From this "tradition", new covenant and new message, flow certain practical consequences for individual community life.

This ecclesiology has certain elements in harmony with Paul's, specifically an eschatology and certain practical consequences flowing from a doctrine of the Church. (This resemblance certainly accounts, in part, for a later tradition to attribute this treatise to Paul.) However the combination of historicity and a certain separateness imply a kind of selectiveness in this view of the Church which is not prominent in Paul and is at some variance with the Synoptics.

5. The Church of the Pastoral Letters.

The Church and its features presented in the Pastoral Letters is a very different one from any of the preceding. First of all, the question of continuity with Judaism is ignored, although continuity seems to be presupposed. Then a settled Church is presented, an "almost-institution". Finally there is certainly the emerging definition of some kinds of positions, of authority and subordination, in Church structure.[28]

The picture that these three letters present is one of a completed Church, firmly established. It is solid, a bulwark and a guarantor of truth; and as such has to have an "administration" that reflects both the necessary holiness of life and the proper teaching of doctrine. The Church sees

14

itself here then as a sociological entity, an existing corporate group; this is a much more static, stable concept, institutional rather than dynamic and vital, although dynamism is not lacking. There is a certain social order in the Church, which is compared to a well-ordered house and family.

Nevertheless the emphasis on organization is theological, for this house has a divine foundation (2 Tim. 2:18-19); it is a holy edifice of those who are called to faith. It is this orderly household of faith that is to guarantee true doctrine and hand on the apostolic tradition. Out of this notion of the Church grows the sociologically stable idea of a fairly well-defined institution, stabilized and stabilizing, and arranged in an order by those who have the position of maintaining the integrity of the Church.

In concluding their respective presentations of the ecclesiology of the Pastoral Epistles, both Schweizer and Schnachenburg caution that this theology may indeed be a one-sided or "limit" view of the Church. Due to the nature and purpose of these letters, we should not expect to find a well-rounded ecclesiology in them. However, even if this is a limit ecclesiology, I believe that the ecclesial style represented here is certainly somewhat different from any of the other ecclesiologies that we find represented in the New Testament.

6. The Johannine Church.

As with the Pastorals, the Church in the Gospels and Letters of John is a "limit" Church, a Church that is in a certain sense a one-sided conception, "historically necessary in face of the danger of the consolidation of the institutional Church."[29] Yet the Church in Johannine theology bears a complexity and richness comparable to Paul's, even if there are probably hints of the

15

polemic against proto-gnosticism. Because of
its complexity and depth, the Johannine material
cannot be considered on the same level as the
Pastorals, because "limit" ecclesiology applies
in quite a different way here.

The first theological contrast with most other
ecclesiologies of the New Testament is the break
with Israel. While "Israel's election is not
denied,"[30] the Church is not a saved remnant
or a renewed Israel. In fact, just the opposite,
for Israel is the prototype of the rejecting world
that in its hostility to God and his Christ sits
in darkness.[31]

Jesus for this evangelist is the Center: He
is the center of God's work, center of the Church
and center of the believer's life. Jesus is the
perfect Gift of God and nothing else is needed
(John 14:7-14). In this view of God's relationship
to man, history is completed; now it is only a
question of making what has happened fruitful
for men. This is what occurs in the Church, for
the Church in this view is composed of those who
are united with Jesus.

This of course leads to the presentation of
an ecclesial theme that is close to Paul's but
expressed in John's terms of a vine (John 15:1-8).
This may be an allusion to the break with Israel:
Jesus is the true Vine that replaces Israel; but
the emphasis is clearly on a deep and abiding
union with Christ and the absolute necessity of
this union. This union is understood to be the
only condition for bearing fruit; lack of union
leads to drastic eschatological consequences.

Two things are to be noted here. First,
although the Church exists in sharp contrast to
the world, it is to bear fruit in the world.
The missionary interest of both Gospel (cf.
Chap. 4) and Epistle is unmistakable, even though
neither are primarily missionary works. The Church
bears a relationship to the world at least insofar

16

as it is bound to give witness to the world and
in the world. This witness to the Supreme Gift,
Jesus, will ultimately bring forth the fruits of
his work wherever the Father wills.

Nevertheless, and this is the second point in
relation to the Vine-allegory, everything is already
completed. The eschatological condition already
exists because the Father's Will is completed
in Jesus; it is only the application of this,
bringing forth fruit, that is to continue for a
time. History does not cease; but the development
of the Church is the continuance of what is already
present and has been accomplished.

This continuance is guaranteed by the Spirit.
The Spirit makes the work of Jesus successful in
and through the Church. It is the Spirit who
works and effects because the Spirit is the Spirit
of union with Jesus. Thus the Church lives with
the Spirit's annointing (1 John 2:20) and the
Gift of both Church and Church members is only
the Spirit. Thus this Spirit alone is the source
of unity among the 'churches', not the sharing
of gifts, spiritual or material; for the one Gift
is from God and this is the surety of unity.
Acceptance of the Gift means union with Jesus
and so with all other believers; rejection leads
to annhilation. Exclusive dependence on Jesus
and his Gift are emphasized in John, not subsidiary
dependence on each other, a prominent theme in
Paul.

But there is no question that this unity in
the Spirit, strongly stressed in John, has certain
consequences, chief of which is love. This
profound, encompassing love is the singular mark
of those who are united with and dependent upon
Jesus. This love is willing to bear suffering
for the sake of the Church (brotherly love is crucial
for the Church), and more important, even for the
sake of a rejecting world. For nowhere is it more
clearly stated that Jesus (and by implication
the Church) gives Himself for the sake of the
world than in Johannine theology. The world is

17

the object of God's salvific activity; the end
has dawned for the world, its choice is to become
Church in union with Jesus, or reject the Gift
and be cast into exterior darkness.

Brief mention should be made here of the
ecclesiology of Revelation (Apocalypse).[32] There
is no question that it is a work that is almost
entirely about the Church. And this Church, like
that of other Johannine writings, is the company
of those who have accepted the Gift of God and
the Revelation made in and through Jesus. But
this Church is more oriented toward the future,
toward fulfillment. There seems to be exhortation
and encouragement to endure in faith, to persevere
to the end. Two prominent ways that seem to bring
this about are, first the identification of the
present suffering Church with the Church in the
heavenly, glorified community. Those who are
now suffering are by that fact already in the
company of the Saints. Secondly, and related
to this, the interior, glorified Church, already
sharing in the Lamb's reward, is described as
the real Church, invisible to the unbelieving,
rejecting world, but present and visible to those
who believe.

Finally and of great importance, this Church
is a Church of martyrs and prophets. Martyrdom
and prophecy are the marks and actions of the
Church and of its members. The Church, suffering
in the wilderness, proclaims continuously the
victory of the Lamb who was slain, and the sure
anticipation of its own manifest glorification
and certain victory. The book itself is just
such a prophetic proclamation, the same kind
of proclamation that is enjoined upon all the believing
Saints.

CONCLUSION

This excursion through ecclesiological inter-
pretations of the New Testament writings could
lead in many directions. But my purpose has not

been to uphold any or all of these ecclesiologies
and ecclesial forms either as normative for today
or even as existing today. I do think that
there is a sense in which they are normative;
and certainly there are certain limits outside
of which the Church ceases to be the Church.
Marcionism and Gnosticism would certainly be
examples from early Church history. At the same
time, Schweizer makes a case for legitimate
divergence outside the New Testament Canon.

Nor do I want to make an "ecumenical case",
at least not in the ordinary sense that this might
be taken today. I am not concerned here with
tracing the development of different conceptions
of the Church through Church history. Probably a
case can be made for the persistence of these
theologies: for example, some might argue that
the Matthean tradition crystalizes around Leo I
and in the canonical tradition of the Roman
Catholic Church, while the Pauline tradition
finds expression and development in the Lutheran
movement and confessions. But historical
ecumenicity is not the point of this monograph.

Rather my concern here has been to establish
a kind of "negative norm". "In the New Testament
Church, there are side by side in the same geographical area groups with a quite different
form, phenomenologically speaking."[33] Because
there were a plurality of forms evidenced in the
New Testament, we should not be uncomfortable
today with the thought of a pluriform Church.
Because we may have inherited fixed ideas of what
the Church should be and do, not only from theology
but also from the social and behaviorial sciences,
it may be difficult to see the need or justification
for such a pluriform Church. But if we examine
the social system in our contemporary society,
we see that various alterations in the social
system itself have developed that have made
our society in many ways different from preceding
ones. These differences have altered the sociological status of religion. The Church has

responded to the social dialectic in a practical way; now we are concerned with _praxis_. For we have not only to consider the social order in the following chapters but a theological ecclesiology as well for a pluriform Church. A polystructured Church in practice must have a pluriform ecclesiology to support it. Certainly Schweizer's conclusion about the Church of the New Testament period may be applicable today: "We cannot escape the plain statement of fact -- that Churches lived side by side which regarded themselves differently on essential points, and which therefore adopted a very different order."34

REFERENCES

1. Other religions, certainly, are rich and articulated, e.g., Islam Hinduism; but they are not our concern here as this is not a study in the philosophy of religion but in the theology of the Church.

2. Raymond E. Brown, S.S., describes this "continuity" thus: "If we are to speak of continuity in New Testament theology, it must be in terms of the Spirit of Christ which constantly brought out the meaning of Jesus, His words and works, for the new circumstances, times and places in which His followers found themselves." New Testament Essays. New York: Doubleday Image Books, 1968. p. 64. (In "The Unity and Diversity in New Testament Ecclesiology", Novum Testamentum, VI, 1963. p. 301.)

3. Ernst Käsemann is talking of "discontinuous "development" when he writes: "Where Gentiles become disciples without previously becoming (Jewish) proselytes, it is not possible to talk seriously of the renewed people of God, but only of the new in antithesis to the old." New Testament Questions of Today. Philadelphia: Fortress Press, 1969. p. 253. (In "Unity and Diversity in New Testament Ecclesiology", Novum Testamentum, VI, 1963. p. 291.) Both Brown's and Kasemann's statements were made to the Fourth World Conference on Faith and Order in Montreal, July, 1963.

4. Käsemann, Ernst, op. cit., p. 252. (Article in Novum Testamentum, p. 290.)

5. Schmidt, K. L., "ἐκκλησία" in Theological Dictionary of the New Testament, Vol. III. Kittel, Gerhard (ed.) Grand Rapids: Wm. B. Eerdman's Publishing Co., 1965. p. 514.

6.   The description that follows is dependent on Schnackenburg, Rudolf, The Church in the New Testament. New York: Herder and Herder, 1965. pp. 17-21.

7.   Schweizer, Eduard. Church Order in the New Testament. London: SCM Press, 1961. Further references to this monograph will list both section number (as Schweizer requests) and pagination in the English translation. 3m (p. 46 in English translation.)

8.   Ibid.

9.   Cerfaux, Lucien. The Church in the Theology of St. Paul. Translated by Geoffrey Webb and Adrian Walker. New York: Herder & Herder, 1959. p. 81, note 65. The internal quote is from Gogul, M. "Unité et diversité du Christianisme primitif", in Revue d'Histoire et de Philisophie Religiouse XIX (1939). p. 19.

10.   Schweizer points out that Stephen and "the seven" were not "table waiters", but seem to be missionary preachers and theologians with "special insight into the new nature of the Church." op. cit. 3o (p. 49 in English translation)

11.   Brown, Raymond, S.S., op. cit., p. 65 (Article in Novum Testamentum, p. 302.)

12.   Schweizer, Eduard, op. cit. Schnackenburg, Rudolf, op. cit. While subsequent New Testament studies over the past ten years would modify in some ways individual conclusions of both Schweizer and Schnackenburg, the overall division, treatment and basic theses of both scholars that concern this subject are still upheld.

13. My subdivisions correspond closely to the subdivisions of both Schweizer and Schnackenburg.

14. Schweizer, 3b (pp. 35-36); Schnackenburg, p. 60.

15. Schweizer, Section 3 (pp. 34-50); Schnackenburg, pp. 56-62.

16. Cf. Schweizer, Section 5 (pp. 63-76); Schnackenburg, pp. 62-69.

17. Schweizer, Section 5n (p. 75) states: "The present time has become central." My own opinion is that Luke remains ambivalent: the focus in his "apocalypse" (Chap. 21) seems to be on the present situation in history; but in his Last Supper discourse, he records those mysterious statements of Jesus which seem to concentrate on the eschatological, viz., 22:16: 18: 28-30. This is why I would say the present is coming into focus as central in Luke's view of history.

18. Cf. Schweizer, Section 4 (pp. 51-62); Schnackenburg, pp. 69-77.

19. Schweizer, 4c (pp. 55).

20. Schweizer (and also Schnackenburg at least by implication) thinks that the law is not "finished and closed". This is the unique position that Peter occupies: he also is to provide an exposition of the law for the Church as new situations occur, cf. 4f (p. 59). But Schweizer notes, as would be expected, the danger of casuistry and legalism.

21. Cf. e.g., Cerfaux, The Church in the Theology of St. Paul, cited in ftnt. 9 and Robinson, John A. T., The Body - A Study in Pauline Theology. London: SCM Press, 1952.

22. Schweizer, 7e (p. 96); Schnackenburg, p. 79.

23. Schweizer, 7d (p. 95); cf. Schnackenburg, pp. 158-165.

24. Schweizer, Section 9 (pp. 110-112); Schnackenburg, pp. 85-89.

25. Schweizer, 9a (p. 110).

26. Sporri, T. Der Gemeindegedanke im ersten Petrusbrief (1925) p. 218, "For him (the author) Christ represents the comprehensive basis and single and decisive beginning and ground, the only sociological point of reference of the community." Quoted in Schnackenburg, p. 211, n. 51. Cf. also Schweizer, 9a (p. 111).

27. Schnackenburg, p. 92. The one theme in Hebrews that doesn't fit as well with "pilgrim people" is the Church as the House of God. For the section on Hebrews, cf. Schnackenburg, pp. 89-92; Schweizer, Section 10 (pp. 113-116).

28. Even Schweizer admits this, although his monograph is a polemic against "episcopal succession" in the Primitive Church. "There is no doubt that (various) regulated ministries do exist." Ftnt. 32o, 6g (p. 84). For the Pastorals, see Schweizer, Section 6 (pp. 77-88); Schnackenburg, pp. 94-102.

29. Schweizer, 12e (p. 130).

30. Schweizer, 11b (p. 119).

31. Thus, what appear to be anti-Jewish statements in the Gospel of John probably should be regarded as "archetypal" judgments on all of unbelieving humanity.

32. Schweizer has three sections for "John's conception of the Church", Section 11, the Gospel (pp. 117-124); Section 12, the Johannine Letters (pp. 125-130); and Section 13, Revelation (pp. 131-136). He thinks that the Church of Revelation is "quite different" from the Church of the Gospel and Letters. Schnackenburg discusses the "Johannine writings, including the Apocalypse" on pp. 103-117. Obviously he believes there is greater continuity between Revelation and the other, traditionally related, Johannine writings.

33. Schweizer, 14b (p. 138).

34. Ibid.

PART   II.

SOCIOLOGICAL   ANALYSIS.

CHAPTER 2

THE DESCRIPTION OF SOCIO-CULTURAL PLURALISM.

The gradual appearance of pluralism in
Western culture is a new phenomenon unknown in this
form anywhere or at any other time. Surely there
have always been those who rejected the institutional forms or the value patterns of their
environing cultures; and certainly also there has
never been complete articulation between social
institutions and the overarching legitimating
schemes that encompassed previous societies.

Today however the situation has changed. It
is not that there is imperfect articulation among
various institutions; there is none, (although
cf. infra, Chap. 3), and no apparent need for any.
No correlation is present. Members of this
society are, more and more, constructing their own
system of values, based on the "market model"
described by Peter Berger. This independent
value construction establishes not only a different
theoretical base for the individual's encounter
with ultimate reality; it inevitably alters the
institutional arrangement of those institutions
connected with value construction, notably religious
institutions. As Parsons pointed out in an early
essay,[1] "a fundamental role in (social) action is
played by normative elements." As the normative
elements or values, the theoretical base, are
changed, so also social action and the institutions
which are the loci for social action will not only
take on a different character; they may and most
probably will also assume a different form. In
this society, life has become an "infinite
possibility thing",[2] and if Bellah's anthropological
analysis is correct, then a new form of religious
institutionalization is the inevitable outcome.

How can we best describe this social phenomenon called "pluralism"? Pluralism is usually

29

described as the co-existence of different ethnic, religious and ideological groups in modern society. It is a co-existence that allows a certain measure of conflict but which (at least until now) moderates that conflict so as to prevent the disintegration of the pluralistic society.

Robin Williams believes that agreement among divergent individuals or groups in modern society, particularly American society, is not maintained about means or even about goals; rather agreement is about processes.[3] But procedural agreement, Williams argues, is not "an agreement about form only";[4] it is an agreement about substance, about the foundational sociological question of order in the society. It is agreement upon process that allows order to be preserved in the pluralistic web of divergent interests and conflicting values.

More narrowly, then, pluralism is a social re-structuring of the ways that the meaning of order in everyday life have significance and value for the members of a society that is described as "pluralistic". This is restructuring of the order of economics, politics, religion, kinship structure, etc. so that all of these "institutions" in such a society have taken on a different and in fact independent structure. They no longer depend for their legitimation on a single over-arching value scheme or interpretive system, a "sacred canopy". Each institution has its own built-in legitimation or justification as well as its first principles, and thus has become auton-omous. Further on in this chapter we shall describe this process for selective major institutions.

This is such a drastic change in social structure that further details regarding its description are necessary. For pluralism represents a change not only in the social structure but even in the institutional patterns of society.[5] For example, not only is the relationship between, say, the economic and political institutions of a society altered, but the very structure of the institutions themselves is changed.

First the question of legitimation or justification of the institution should be considered.
In previous social groups, there has been a single
"official" over-arching legitimating scheme,
usually a religious one, into which the major
social institutions fit.[6]   Classical civilization
gives us the clearest model of this. The state,
the family, warfare, economic policy, religion and
whatever else all fit somehow into a "sacred cosmos"
and were in fact justified by that "sacred view
of the world". But we needn't look to Egypt or
Rome for our paradigm. As late as the 19th century
Karl Marx's theory of economic determinism was a
kind of "sacred canopy", if a para-religious one,[7]
that sought to justify and/or legitimate state,
family, war, revolution, a-religion and the future
itself. But today this kind of over-arching world-
view has in fact broken down, a process already
begun in Marx's day. Each institution in society is
independently capable of providing its own justification. The state, the economy or the family
need no "will of God" or "historical dialectic"
to justify their existence and operation.

There is another dimension of pluralism that
should be considered. Not only do modern institutions need no external justification, they also
depend on themselves for their own first principles
of "social action". The basis or root of each of
these fundamental institutions is in its own
operation and existence. The first principles of
economics simply do not apply to aesthetics,Marx
and dialectical materialism to the contrary.
Which principles are first and which are second or
derivative depend on the institution that is being
investigated. In previous social systems, a set
of first principles was either assumed or explicitly
developed as underlying the whole social fabric.
Indeed, philosophy as often as not has been described
as a search for just such first principles.

In a pluralistic world, things are manifestly
different. The principles that apply to scientific

31

investigation are not those that, on the face of
it, are considered first in economics. This new
world is a very different experience from any
previous social configuration. And it has given
rise to a new structure in each of society's
institutions. What has actually happened in these
major institutions is what we must investigate.

The following individual investigation of
institutions is not a haphazard arrangement.
Rather, the order has been deliberately chosen to
indicate both a rough chronology and a sort of
structural-causal pattern. These institutions
shouldn't be thought of as dominoes that keel
over, one after another, as each successively
moves out from under the "sacred canopy". Rather
there is a complex structure of institutions that
influence each other and later the shape of society
in the process as each moves toward its own kind
of autonomy. The greater complexity in a society
leads to a

> more heterogeneous social distribution of
> the world view... At a certain level of
> complexity of the social structure the
> social and occupational stratification
> leads to typical differences in social-
> ization which also affect the acquisition
> of sacred knowledge. The resulting
> inequality in the distribution of religious
> representations will induce, at the very
> least, the consolidation of different
> versions of the sacred cosmos among
> occupational groups and social strata.[8]

Complexity, in Luckmann's view, leads inevitably
to "religious pluralism", and given the forces
and tensions of the modern world, to a socio-
cultural pluralism that has altered the shape of
modern religion.

This investigation begins by taking Luckmann's
criticism seriously:

> The new sociology of religion badly
> neglected its theoretically most signi-
> ficant task: to analyze the changing --
> not necessarily institutional -- basis
> of religion in modern society.[9]

Thus the concern here is not that religious
organizations take on the same bureaucratic structures
as modern economic and political organizations
(although they certainly have[10]) but rather that
the whole socio-structural base of religion has
drastically altered in the modern world. Pluralism
seems a good way of describing this alteration.

POLITICAL INSTITUTIONS

The first institution to move out from under
the "sacred canopy" was the political one. The
tension between political reality and the province
claimed by the "sacred", manifest in Church-Empire
conflicts in Western Christendom, and Caesaropapism
in Eastern, finally led to the separation of a
distinct, self-justifying political order beginning
with the rupture between Philip the Fair of France
and Boniface VIII. Boniface insisted on the
exclusive competency of the "sacred canopy" as
manifested in the "official" legitimating structures
of the Church, but Philip had already moved out
from under this "official" canopy, as would so many
others with the rise of national states. It was
Jean Bodin in the 16th century who first gave
systematic utterance to the autonomy of political
institutions: "La souverainete est la puissance
absolue et perpetuelle d'une Republique." This
notion of autonomy has been developed from Bodin
through Hobbes, Rousseau and Hegel; and it is
still the firm foundation of nationhood in the
spectrum from social and liberal democracies to
military totalitarianism.

What has been the modern result, and what
are the institutional facts about political autonomy?

Political society is now seen in the modern
world as having its own purpose, which is the
construction of a just and harmoniously integrated
social order. It is based on its own first principles which are justice and law. "Justice is the
primary condition for the existence of the body
politic ... Every kind of law, from spontaneous,
unformulated group regulation to customary law and
to law in the full sense of the term, contributed
to the vital order of political society."[11]
Justice and integration are the goals for political
institutions, the same goals that religion, especially
in Christianity and Islam, have set up for themselves. And the first principles of the political
order are justice and law. This is not to maintain that these are the only concerns or areas
that touch political life, but rather that these
first principles and purposes establish the autonomy
of political reality. The political institution
has become specialized and needs no further justification.

The Church itself has recognized that social
justice is achieved by political bodies. At the
Fourth Assembly of the World Council of Churches
in 1968, the Report on World Economic and Social
Development urged many tasks upon churches and
their members. But the task of achieving social
justice was a "political task" that mainly concerned the activities of governments. Article 38
of that report states that Churches should bring
their influence to bear on 1) political parties
and 2) governments themselves.[12] Thus the Churches
themselves acknowledge that the primary responsibility in the task of achieving social justice is
not theirs but the body politic.

Thus the body politic, the political institutionalization in a society, is seen as an all-
pervasive organ which fosters and supports what
is called by political philosophers the "common
good". Political scientists prefer the terms
"public interest", but definitely identify the
two.[13] Maritain described the common good in
this way:

The common good is not only the collection of public commodities and services which the organization of common life presupposes: a sound fiscal condition, a strong military force; the body of just laws, good customs and wise institutions which provides the political society with its structure; the heritage of its great historical remembrances, its symbols and its glories, its living traditions and cultural treasures. The common good also includes the sociological integration of all the civic conscience, political virtues and sense of law and freedom, of all the activity, material prosperity and spiritual riches, of unconsciously operating hereditary wisdom, of moral rectitude, justice, friendship, happiness, virtue and heroism in the individual lives of the members of the body politic. To the extent to which all these things are, in a certain measure, <u>communicable</u> and revert to each member, helping him to perfect his life and liberty as a person, they all constitute the good human life of the multitude.[14]

As this has become more consciously and reflexively the object of deliberate choice, we find the political body assuming its own <u>raison d'etre</u> and having its own first principles. Following from this seem to be the goals of the preservation of order, the promotion of justice and the establishment of peace based on certain minimal and consensual standards of "public morality."[15]

More interesting than the speculative work of theoreticians, however, is the actual view of populations on their conception of the "government". It is the government that establishes basic moral attitudes, preserves order (and hence maintains the social system), promotes justice with special concerns about social justice and seeks peace. (Cf. e.g., the Preamble to the Constitution of the United States.) All of these without exception were formerly associated, although not always exclusively, with religious functions and in fact most often with institutional forms of religion.

A sampling of recent public opinion polls indicates the common attitude toward the activity of the government. Three areas that have been associated with religion have been morality, even public morality, justice including social justice, and rights, especially civil rights. In the areas of morality, in 1965, 77% of the adults asked favored a curfew for children under 16.[16] In 1970, 91% of Americans wants Congress to appropriate more money to help police and other law enforcement agencies deal with crime.[17] And finally in 1975, 69% favored laws requiring stricter handgun control, and even 48% were in favor of stricter control over rifles and shotguns.[18]

This last brings us into the area of "rights" as well as of morality. In the case of civil rights, in 1964, 71% of whites outside the South favored the passage of a law giving blacks the rights to be served and accommodated in public places.[19] And in the broader area of social justice, similar results have been found by Evelyn Ogren,

> Most respondents (76 percent) believed that American society has an obligation to keep the poor from living a substandard life .... There was also wide agreement (76 percent) that the children of the poor should be provided with the kind of childhood that will pull them out of poverty, even if their unworthy parents have to be supported to do so.[20]

Further and more elaborate testimony could be provided; but the issue seems clear. Law as moral

determinant and justice belong principally if
not exclusively to the domain of the State. What
is surprising is not that people want the "government"
to do these things, but that such overwhelming
majorities want the government to be source and
guardian of justice and morality. This, coupled
with the growing belief that religion is losing its
influence on American life,21 indicates rather
strongly that institutionalized religion is no
longer perceived as the preserver of order or source
of justice. Rather the body politic has these
functions and is autonomous in exercising them.

Thus, citizens in a western democracy, like
the United States, obviously regard the state as
having certain specific tasks and obligations and
holding an imperative to fulfill them independently
of any other sourc or mandate. This is the
autonomy that an institution acquires as it no
longer seeks shelter under the sacred canopy. What
does autonomy mean and is it paradigmatic for
other institutions in society?

> The relation of the individual to the
> state demonstrates the distinctive nature
> of the political monopoly of power. For
> the individual's allegiance to the state,
> unlike his membership in a labor union or
> a church, cannot easily be transferred; and
> he can resign from citizenship only at the
> cost of resigning from the whole society
> at the same time. That the status of citi-
> zen is a primary base for a series of other
> statuses is shown by the contemporary plight
> of large numbers of stateless persons who
> exist by sufferance within alien and often
> hostile nations or in international enclaves
> .... Thus the state's monopoly of authority
> renders the rights and duties of citizens
> a matter of special interest to each indivi-
> dual - and to the sociology of political
> behavior.22

It is this status of citizen that is important in
understanding the prototype of the autonomous

institution. Unlike feudal society or the medieval empire, where citizenship in a particular duchy or even nation was not so determinative of status, now citizenship in a particular state qualifies and allows a number of other statuses; and without citizenship there are simply a number of roles, tasks, positions, etc. that an individual becomes "incapable" of. Thus the state takes on a definite autonomy and is capable of creating and determining for individuals aspects of the significant world independent of any other justifying or integrating institution.

All of this is no longer dependent on a specifically religious orientation or church affiliation. Lenski, for instance, discovered "the irrelevance of doctrinal orthodoxy for most aspects of secular life".[23] He reports this specifically in the context of the relationship of belief to certain political positions. Religious beliefs and church affiliation are only two, and not the most significant, among several variables influencing people's political values and persuasion; and conversely, "politics and religion don't mix" axiomatically in modern society. Brian Wilson talks of the "relative marginality of religious issues to the political parties in the secular society".[24]

No intent is made here to deny any correlation between religion and political attitudes.[25] What is the intent of this section is to demonstrate that the political order has established its own domain, that it is not perceived as having received a mandate from some divine integrating plan nor is it dependent on such a plan for its own justification. The political order has broken out from under the "sacred canopy", and so the Reformation axiom, "cujus regio, illius religio" could be viewed as a violation and infringement of the individual's personal and private affairs.

THE ECONOMY AS A SOCIAL INSTITUTION

There is no question that in the Western world the economy as a social institution has developed

its own set of principles, goals and justifications.
Weber's insistence on the essentially "profane"
nature of economic activity in the West led him to
consider the relation of religion to the economy
in many societies. However, "the commercialization
of property and labor, which was essential to the
development of modern capitalism is, historically
speaking, a recent and extreme development."[26]
This style of economic institutionalization leads
to a "relatively complete separation of the economic
uses of goods, services, human beings and other
means of production from all their other uses . . .
Above all, the treatment of labor as a commodity
necessitates separating economic considerations
from traditional social obligations and ethical
sentiments".[27]

The business creed emphasizes "sheer productivity
and efficiency in itself". This is the first
principle in economic life, "emphasis on production
for its own sake",[28] i.e., provide more and
different things for more people at less cost. The
economy looks no further for its first principles:
high per capita productivity and low cost per unit.
Behind these basic principles of economic life
seems to lie the conviction (at least in the United
States) that "private, free enterprise and the
ownership and enjoyment of property is embedded in
the Constitution of the United States".[29]

The justifying rationale for this, as claimed by
the spokesmen for economic institutions, is to
serve the community at large and to provide equality
of opportunity for all who want to avail themselves
of the system. However, like so many self-justifying
rationalizations, this one has not been statistically
examined nor subjected to processes of verification by
those who want to bolster these economic institutions.

The goals of a separate economic system in a
pluralistic situation are more amenable to verification.
"Among the aspirations of the American people, no
other is so universally proclaimed as a high level
of consumption. By this is meant an abundance of

goods and services that flow from labor, natural resources, and capital. . . " [30] This high level of consumption is certainly evident in the western world and has become the focus of Americanized economic goals for the world.

> The major world economic goals are accepted as being the following efforts: (1) rising per capita productivity and production, particularly where these are lowest, thus contributing to (2) greater equality and justice among nations in the distribution of the world's production while maintaining (3) maximum freedom of economic choice for the individual, both as consumer and producer.[31]

This level of consumption as the economic goal for the population at large means a transformation of the economic goals (and implicitly economic structures). In a section of The Decline of Radicalism, subtitled "From Wealth to Standard of Living", historian Daniel S. Boorstin astutely observes: "Wealth is by definition what a man possesses. Property is what is 'proper' to a person, peculiar or special to him. How obvious, then, that the wealth of some should explain the poverty of others. . . .

But standard of living is what a man shares. One man's standard of living cannot be sharply separated from that of others. Each person is part of everyone else's standard of living. You are my environment. And my environment is my standard of living."[32]

By environment, Boorstin means the ready availability of all the goods and services that a consumption economy can provide plus freedom from threat of crime, educational availability, clean air and water, roads, public transportation and wide opportunities. None of these things are readily present if the goal of the economic system is wealth. It is only when "material achievements - especially

40

the high and rising standard of living - take first place,"[33] that the economic system offers a goal possibly accessible to all. For as Boorstin points out in this suggestive passage, the standard of living becomes the communal goal binding all together in a redundantly self-justifying economic system. The economy is a separate system of ordering, principles, standards and goals; like so many other institutions in our society, it does not look beyond itself for its justification or order.

The change in the structure of economic institutions is generally conceded to be the movement away from home or family-centered enterprise to work for another that takes the wage-earner away from the hearth, home and family. The model for the former is alleged to be the family farm; and for the latter, the alienating corporate enterprise. Perhaps the heritage of Marx is too strong, and this structural change has been accepted as the alienating agent in modern society; but there is no conclusive evidence to support this. Certainly many occupations before the advent of industrialization took workers out of their homes, e.g., finance, tradesmen, several crafts that meant employment of journeymen in the workshops of master craftsmen. Even much farming was done by workers who lived within the confines of a town or village, going out to the farm at dawn and returning to town, home and family at twilight.

The difference is not principally that of home vs. away-from-home occupation. The difference is the ordering principle which has changed because of a structural change, different than the one usually advanced as explanatory. The first distinguishing feature of modern economic institutions is their size. John Glover makes the case for this feature as the distinguishing element in our civilization: it is the large technological enterprise, the enterprise that engages over 500 persons in cooperative productive activity. Certainly this is a new economic structure that significantly alters the ordering principles of the economy. It is no longer relationships to individuals but to institutions, no longer

41

personal responsibility and integrity but rules and regulations that govern behavior, no longer primary-type relationships but secondary, and no longer consideration of position in the social order but the economic institution that carries weight in <u>the institution</u> <u>itself</u>. The structure and the self-justifying rationale mutually influence one another. Other institutions have followed this model: large urban high schools, the corporation farm, welfare and charitable agencies, to name a few.[34]

Resulting from and connected with this first structural change is a second: the increase in geographical or spatial mobility. Workers in significant numbers were and are willing to move in order to be engaged in working in the large, corporate productive enterprise. For obvious economic reasons, individuals are willing to cut off from their roots in the social order and to accept the structural and rational self-justification of economic institutions. This is the pattern that was reported in industrializing England, the pattern evident in industrializing countries today and in the United States. In this country, the percent of males, 20 - 64 years old, whose fathers were farm workers but who as of 1962 live in nonfarm residence is 76.8%, i.e., 76.8% of a large sample (over 12 million) have left the farm in the space of one generation.[35] This kind of male geographical mobility certainly has a major relationship to occupation and economic activity. It would seem to be an indicator that the economic institution as a whole has its own independent system, even for a population traditionally considered the most conservative in a society, those with a farm background.

The self-justifying rationale for economic activity, efficiency and productivity has produced, directly as well as indirectly, profound changes in the size and composition of the occupational structure. We can see how the workers themselves have actually adopted the economic rationale for their economic activities. A brief review of

42

these dramatic changes will point up the attitudinal changes in the working population.

The most impressive change seems to be the drop in workers engaged in farm occupations: 72% in 1820, about 37% in 1900, and 6.3% in 1960 in the United States.[36]   However, the most telling change in occupational structure, only indicated by the drop in agricultural employment, is the switch from the production of physical goods to the providing of services. At the beginning of the century, 73.3% were engaged in production, both farm and non-farm. In 1960, "only 46% of the workers were engaged in the actual production of physical goods."[37]   The implications of 54% of the working population engaged in service activities as economic activity have yet to be fully explored. For purposes of this discussion, though, it surely highlights the fact that "service" is to be subsumed under and justified by the economic rationale, not by appeals to a more general ethic of service to fellow man, the building up of the commonwealth or of the Kingdom of God.

This new direction in terms of the pluralistic segmentation of the population in the United States becomes more evident in a closer examination of the work force.

In analyzing characteristics of the farm and non-farm population in the United States, Beale and his collaborators found that 63.4% of those born on farms had become members of the non-farm population. Strangely enough, percentages increased with increase in age. Of those 18 to 24 years of age, 53% of the farm born had moved away from the farm. For those 25 to 64, the average percentage was about 63.5%; but for those over 65 the percentage was 68.1%.[38]   More striking than this well-known statistic of movement off the farms is another finding of Beale: of those still living on farms, about one-third (34.4%) are not engaged in agricultural occupations.[39]

The reverse move, those who move from non-farm to farm residence, is insignificantly small, 3.2%

of those "non-farm born". Even so, only about half of these are in agricultural occupations (47.4% of a total labor force of 1,466,000 movers from non-farm to farm).[40]

Blau and Duncan found even greater disparity in occupation between farmers and their sons. In 1947, 38% of sons of farmers were themselves working on farms; in 1952, 34%; in 1957, 26%; and by 1962, 22%.[41] The implication of this is that the farm labor force decreased by about 42% in 15 years.

This move from farm to non-farm occupations and residence can be seen as motivated mainly by economic considerations. It is simply more profitable personally to work at other than agricultural occupations and no amount of other ties or commitments can keep them "down on the farm".

Another important indication that economic considerations have their own value sets is evident in the change of occupations from father to son. Blau and Duncan note that:

> The three occupational groups that manifest most occupational inheritance and self-recruitment are the only three that entail self-employment - independent professionals, proprietors and farmers. It seems that proprietorship -- of a farm a business, or a professional practice -- discourages sons from leaving the occupation of their fathers and makes it difficult for other men to move into an occupation.[42]

Great occupational mobility is evident even in broad classification. Blau and Duncan, in their review of surveys at five year intervals, found that at least 30% of sons were not even in the same general occupational groups, white-collar or manual, as their fathers. This inter-generational occupational mobility, of course is much higher, 78%,

44

for farmers.43   In a more detailed occupational
breakdown, it can be seen that less than a third
of the respondents follow directly in their father's
footsteps. (See Table 1, p. 46.) I have under-
lined the corresponding occupation to make the
mobility more evident. In percentages, this
breaks down to each occupation, except farmers,
recruiting at least 85% of their personnel
from different origins.

Occupational mobility takes another form as
well. The individual male wage-earner in about
forty-five years of working life on the average
changes jobs about 10 times and changes occupations
4 times. While this can be interpreted in various
ways, there is no doubt that it does mean a high
degree of job mobility for the worker. This mobility
may in large part be horizontal, but it points to
the fact that there are no traditional ties, no
loyalties that hold the inividual to any place or
kind of employment. Thus, we can conclude with
Robin Williams' statement that was already quoted
that there is

> (R)elatively complete separation of
> the economic uses of goods, services, human
> beings and other means of production from
> all these other uses . . . . Above all,
> the treatment of labor as a commodity nec-
> essitates separating economic considerations
> from traditional social obligations and
> ethical sentiments.44

One final fact that relates to the economic
structure is geographical mobility. Consistently
since the end of World War II, 20% of the population
over one year old moves annually. (See Table 2,
p. 48.) This kind of geographic movement can best
be interpreted as having both economic motivation and
rationalization. It can safely be assumed that
most poeple who move out of the county (technically,
migrants) are in search of a better economic
situation, or have already found it; while many of
those who remain within the same county but move

TABLE 1

MOBILITY FROM FATHER'S OCC. TO 1962 OCC., FOR MALES 25 TO 64 YEARS OLD: OUTFLOW PERCENTAGES

Father's Occupation	RESPONDENT'S OCCUPATION IN MARCH, 1962																	TOTAL
	1	2	3	4	5	6	7	8	9	10	11	12	13	14	15	16	17	
1 Professionals Self Empl.	16.7	31.9	9.9	9.5	4.4	4.0	1.4	2.0	1.8	2.2	2.6	1.6	1.8	.4	2.2	2.0	.8	100.0
2 Salaried	3.3	31.9	12.9	5.9	4.8	7.6	1.7	3.8	4.4	1.0	6.9	5.2	3.4	1.0	.6	.8	.2	100.0
3 Managers	3.5	22.6	19.4	6.2	7.9	7.6	1.1	5.4	5.3	3.1	4.0	2.5	1.5	1.1	.8	.5	.1	100.0
4 Salesmen,Other	4.1	17.6	21.2	13.0	9.3	5.3	3.5	2.8	5.4	1.9	2.6	3.7	1.7	.0	.8	1.0	.3	100.0
5 Proprietors	3.7	13.7	18.4	5.8	16.0	6.2	3.3	3.5	5.2	3.9	5.1	3.6	2.8	.5	1.2	1.1	.4	100.0
6. Clerical	2.2	23.5	11.2	5.9	5.1	8.8	1.3	6.6	7.1	1.8	3.8	4.6	5.6	1.0	1.8	1.3	.0	100.0
7 Salesmen,Retail	.7	13.7	14.1	8.8	11.5	6.4	2.7	5.8	3.4	3.1	8.8	5.1	4.6	.1	3.1	2.2	.0	100.0
8 Craftsmen Mfg.	1.0	14.9	8.5	2.4	6.2	6.1	1.7	15.3	6.4	4.4	10.9	6.2	4.6	1.7	2.4	.4	.1	100.0
9 Other	.9	11.1	9.2	3.9	6.5	7.6	1.5	7.8	12.2	4.4	8.2	9.2	4.6	1.2	2.8	.9	.3	100.0
10 Construction	.9	6.7	7.1	2.6	8.3	7.9	.8	10.4	8.2	13.9	7.5	6.2	5.2	1.1	4.3	.8	.6	100.0
11 Operatives Mfg.	1.0	8.6	5.3	2.7	5.6	6.0	1.4	12.2	7.3	3.2	17.9	6.9	5.1	4.0	3.5	.8	.8	100.0
12 Other	.6	11.5	5.1	2.5	6.6	6.3	1.4	7.1	9.3	4.9	10.4	12.5	5.9	2.1	4.2	.9	1.1	100.0
13 Service	.8	8.8	7.4	3.5	6.0	9.0	1.9	8.0	6.4	5.4	11.7	8.1	10.5	2.7	3.3	1.0	.2	100.0
14 Laborers Mfg.	.0	6.0	5.3	.7	3.3	4.4	.7	10.7	6.0	2.8	18.1	9.4	9.4	7.1	5.8	1.7	.9	100.0
15 Other	.4	4.9	3.5	2.5	3.5	8.7	1.7	7.7	8.2	5.7	12.7	10.6	8.1	3.4	9.9	.9	1.1	100.0
16 Farmers	.6	4.2	4.1	1.2	6.0	4.3	1.1	5.6	6.7	5.8	10.2	8.6	4.8	2.4	5.4	16.6	3.9	100.0
17 Farm Laborers	.2	1.9	2.9	.6	4.0	3.5	1.2	6.4	6.6	5.8	13.1	10.8	7.5	3.2	9.2	5.7	9.4	100.0
Total	1.4	10.2	7.9	3.1	7.0	6.1	1.5	7.2	7.1	4.9	9.9	7.6	5.5	2.1	4.3	5.2	1.7	100.0

A Rows as shown do not total 100.0, since men not in experienced civilian labor force are not shown separately.

After Blau and Duncan, op. cit., p.28.

46

have an altered economic situation, either for better or worse. What has happened is that many people no longer have a feeling for or attachment to their geographic location. God has not sanctified a particular place for them, nor do they have any intimations that somehow the place where they live is "holy ground". Modern man is in fact only too eager to shake the "dust off his feet" if it leads to his economic advantage.

Another perspective is provided by a Marxist analysis. From the Marxist viewpoint, it is possible to pursue the analysis of pluralization even further. Not only do autonomous principles and goals serve a functional purpose, they also allow certain groups in modern society to pursue their own autonomous economic ends. Those who control the means of production and can deal with and manipulate those who sell their labor share common economic interests and maintain a basic misunderstanding if not hostility toward other groups in the society. This, of course, is a thumbnail description of Marx's view of class structure. Certainly in the Marxist view as well, this separation of economic institutions from the "sacred canopy" leads to a pluralistic situation, at least for the capitalist and entrepreneurial class. And an institution with its own first principles and rationale could discard the restraints of "morality" based on religion, an institution that, for this class, is now separated from the economy.

Marx pursued this line of thought even further, for he believed that just as the capitalist class developed its own first principles, it also encouraged for other classes, especially the working proletariat, the maintenance and continuation of the "sacred canopy". For religion, in the Marxist analysis, keeps a check on the legitimate aspirations of the worker for justice, while its compartmentalization for the capitalist allows his greed to run unbridled. Thus a Marxist analysis brings us, via a separate route, to the same pluralistic dimension of social

47

TABLE 2

Mobility since 1948:
Mobility Statistics for Population 1 Year Old and Over.

	Same Household	Different House in U.S. Same County (Movers)	Different House in Different Count (Migrants)
April 1947 - April 1948	79.8	13.6	6.4
April 1949 - April 1950	80.9	13.1	5.6
April 1954 - April 1955	79.6	13.3	6.6
March 1959 - March 1960	80.1	12.9	6.4
March 1964 - March 1965	79.3	13.4	6.8
March 1968 - March 1969	81.0	11.7	6.6
March 1975 - March 1979*	56.7	22.6	19.3

* (4 years and older)

Source:
  U.s. Bureau of the Census, Current Population Reports
Series P.20. No. 193, "Mobility of the Population
of the United States, March 1968 to March 1969", U.S.
Government Printing Office, Washington, D.C., 1969.

  U.S. Bureau of the Census, Current Population Reports
Series P-20, No. 353, "Geographical Mobility:
March 1975 to March 1979", Table 6.

institutions; for the "infrastructure" has indeed developed its own rationale. In this "radical" analysis, pluralism is seen as beneficial to economic entrepeneurial and property owners, while the "sacred canopy" is imposed on other classes. I believe that we have moved into a post-Marxist situation in which pluralism has touched all classes. However, the non-capitalist classes still do not know how to exploit the pluralistic situation to their own advantage.

In summing up, we may say that this new economic attitude represents a clear and definite departure from the traditional teaching of Christianity at least up to early modern times:

> The counsel of Baxter, Wesley, Fox and Penn -- as well as St. Paul -- in this kind of context includes no admonition to seek advancement and "fight one's way forward", but to remain in the station to which one has been called, industrious, faithful and content with one's lot. Perform your daily tasks without striving for advancement and riches, and devote your free time to serving God and doing good.[45]

Kurt Samuelsson is presenting here what had been the counsel consistently given to those who would traditionally establish their world view around God and His divine order. It is only as that order no longer provides the rationale for every aspect of life, singly and integrally, that the whole order changes and a pluralistic situation arises.

THE FAMILY AS AUTONOMOUS

It is a commonplace to discuss the transformation from the extended family system to the nuclear family unit. However, recent investigation has produced evidence that the basic family pattern,

49

at least in England and the United States, has not changed in ten or twelve generations, but has in fact been nuclear well before the Industrial Revolution.[46]   Yet what is the situation that has caused public worry about the breakdown of the family and sponsored the convocation of conferences and the publication of a multitude of books?

The statistical evidence of marital disintegration is not very encouraging. The ratio of divorces to marriages in the United States has narrowed after World War I, beginning in 1920, as Table 3 clearly shows. (p. 51)

If sociological investigation of family life in previous generations is approximately correct, then transformation from extended to nuclear family is not a factor in the breakdown of marriages and the change in familial living. We must look else-where; and a condition, if not a causal factor, lies in the nature of social pluralism.

The family no longer transmits the global system of values; instead it has become a speciality institution, one alongside many others in our society.[4] The new nuclear family is still an agent of primary socialization, providing the first and perhaps basic interpretation of the universe. But no longer does nor can the family provide the beginning of that global interpretation as do families of more traditional societies. In fact, the world-view provided by the family is complemented and even challenged very early on in the life of the individual, not only by peer-group relationships, but by the bombardment of the media, contact with other institutions in society, especially educational and economic, and the ambivalent attitudes of parents themselves. "Sociologists think that the social situation is responsible for the confusion in the family and not vice versa."[48] And this social confusion leads to confusion about the place of the family in society that is new to the present "pluralistic" situation.

TABLE 3

Marriage and Divorce Rates

	Marriage Rate (per 1000)	Divorce Rate (per 1000)
1920	12.0	1.6
1925	10.3	1.5
1930	9.2	1.6
1935	10.4	1.7
1940	12.1	2.0
1945	12.2	3.5
1950	11.1	2.6
1955	9.3	2.3
1960	8.5	2.2
1965	9.3	2.5
1970	10.7	3.5
1975	10.0	4.8

Sources:
    U. S. Bureau of the Census. Historical Statistics of the United States, 1789-1945. United States Department of Commerce, Washington, D.C., 1949.

    U. S. Bureau of the Census. Historical Statistics of the United States, Colonial Times to 1957. U.S. Department of Commerce, Washington, D.C., 1960.

    U. S. Bureau of the Census. Statistical Abstract of the United States, 1975. (97th edition) U. S. Department of Commerce, Washington, D.C., 1976.

Primarily, the traditional functions of the family have been taken over by other social institutions as they seek their own justifications through providing their own rationale and through functional specialization of institutions. Traditionally, analysis of the family yields seven functional areas that the family fills: economic, educational, religious, recreational, protective, biological and affectional.[49] Parsons condenses these to 1) primary socialization, and 2) stabilization of adult personalities of society.[50] The truth of the matter is that all of these functions are now partially if not wholly in the hands of other agents of socialization or stabilization.

The family has a new function, or if not entirely new, one that has become the central focus of the contemporary family: this is the "gratifying and restoring (of) individuals psychologically by means of primary group life".[51] In 1945, M.C. Elmer described this functional change: "Instead of economic activity, ownership of flocks and herds, occupation or titles, political prestige or genealogical facts or fabrication, mutual affection and sympathetic understanding are becoming the basis of family organization."[52] The basic focus of the family has changed from "an institution to a companionship arrangement"[53] and this change has brought confusion and need for reintegration.

The new function of mutual support, restoration and gratification has taken over; and there are no necessary ties with the rest of society. Primary group life is central in the family in a pluralistic age. This has led to a re-statement of the raison d'etre of the family and to a concomitant autonomy of the family as an institution in society.

The present raison d'etre and justifying first principle of the family is "love". The change from institution to companionship, from "familism to individualism"[54] can be subsumed under the shorthand: "love". This is the new purpose of the family and the chief reason for individuals to seek to form a family: to provide that warm, pro-

52

tective atmosphere possible only in the primary group that serves as a support, restorative and buffer from the challenging complexities of a world that has no unifying center. This is the purpose not only for those individuals who have by their partnership initially formed the social unit; it also serves as the focus for those for whom it is the family of origin, i.e., the children. Child-raising patterns in the United States show a definite trend toward warm, supportive attitudes in the raising of children. Thus, marriage has become companionate not only for those who form the family, but also for those who are born into the family.[55]

That marriage must become more companionate for those who enter and initiate a family is indicated by the statistics presented on Table 4. (p. 54) These would certainly indicate that husbands and wives now and in the projected future will spend many years together after the last child is grown and has left home. Many consequences of this are presented in an unpublished report that I collaborated on.[56]

Because the family has its own internal justification, best described in the shorthand, "love", it has become substantially an autonomous unit in the pluralistic social system. "Perhaps the key term to describe the American family is autonomy. It gives considerable freedom to its members; and the family is relatively autonomous in that it is so loosely integrated into the larger society. Cultural guidelines ... are scanty and vague. The nuclear family ... is cut loose from the supports and restraints which can be offered by a clan or an extended family."[57]   This autonomy I take in the fullest sense: the family is a separate cultural institution outside the "sacred canopy"[58] which needs no further justification than its own internal self-justification; "love", companionship, mutual support and restoration. All are within the social unit itself. There are no pleas to the outside, not even to biology.

53

TABLE 4

Stage in Life Cycle	1890	1940	1950	1959	1980 (projected)
Median Age of Wife at:					
1st Marriage	22.0	21.5	20.1	20.2	19.5-20.4
Birth of Last Child	31.9	27.1	26.1	25.8	27 - 28
Marriage of Last Child	55.3	50.0	47.6	47.1	48 - 49
Death of Husband	53.3	60.9	61.4	63.6	65 - 66
Median Age of Husband at:					
1st Marriage	26.1	24.3	22.8	22.3	22 - 23
Birth of Last Child	36.0	29.9	28.8	27.9	29 - 30
Marriage of Last Child	59.4	52.8	50.3	49.2	51 - 52
Death of Wife	57.4	63.6	64.1	65.7	68 - 69

Source:
Sourcebook in Marriage and the Family, Sussman, M. ed. p. 37. "Stages of Life Cycle of the Family, For the U.S. from 1890-1980". quoted in Feucht, p. 143.

54

This does not mean that the family is dying or on the decline in our pluralistic society. It means rather that new functions, processes and forms characterize the family. Just as other major social institutions did not collapse but have been and are in the process of alteration, so the family is undergoing the same kind of alteration in our society. Traditionalists need not bemoan the end of the family. It is merely suffering the birth pangs of a new beginning.

CONCLUSION

The conclusion to this chapter does not need to be labored. Cetainly we can say that these three institutions, political, economic and familial, seem to occupy a different place in the social order than they did in previous history, specifically in the Christian world, but by implication in other societies as well. Only two points need to be made.

First, these institutions have been chosen because they seem to represent in the minds of sociologists, and by a kind of consensus, the major institutions in society. Luckmann, Inkeles and Lundstorn all seem to agree that these institutions are "foundational" or primary. In speaking of traditional societies, Luckmann observes: "The sacred cosmos permeates the various, more or less clearly differentiated, institutional areas such as kinship, the division of labor and the regulation of the exercise of power."[59]   Such pervasiveness, Luckmann believes and I have tried to indicate, no longer exists.

Secondly, other institutions that could have been presented for investigation here are really derivative, at least in part, from these institutions. Thus, legal institutions, certainly as autonomous as any, are derived from the political order and from the long-term development of political autonomy. Education as an institution, a relatively new institution in the modern social order, is dependent partially upon the economy and partially also upon

the family, as the family's agent and surrogate.
It would seem to follow that these institutions
also would have their own autonomy, adding to the
complexity of the pluralistic situation, and they
too are no longer subject to a religious justification,
a sacred canopy that sanctifies every human activity
to establish its value and relevance for society.

REFERENCES

1. Parsons, Talcott, "The Role of Ideas in Social Action", Essays in Sociological Theory. Glencoe: The Free Press of Glencoe, 1954. p. 29. This essay was first published in 1938.

2. Bellah, Robert N. Beyond Belief. New York: Harper & Row, 1970. p. 40.

3. Williams, Robin M., Jr. American Society. 3rd edition. New York: Knopf, 1970. pp. 235-236.

4. Ibid., p. 236.

5. Cf. Luckmann, Thomas. The Invisible Religion. New York: MacMillan, 1967, especially Chapter 6, "Religion and Personal Identity in Modern Society".

6. Cf. ibid., p. 61. "Religious representations serve to legitimate conduct in the full range of social situations."

7. Cf. Nottingham, Elizabeth. Religion: A Sociological View. New York: Random House, 1971. pp. 25-26.

8. Luckmann, op. cit., pp. 64-65.

9. Ibid., p. 18.

10. Cf. Harrison, Paul M. Power and Authority in the Free Church Tradition. Princeton: Princeton University Press, 1959. pp. x-xi; 135-138; and Berger, Peter. The Sacred Canopy. Garden City: Doubleday Anchor, 1969. pp. 139-141.

11. Maritain, Jacques. Man and the State. Chicago: University of Chicago Press, 1951. pp. 10-11. (Italics mine.) Maritain affirms these principles of an "autonomous" body politic even though he denies the political theory explicitly of Bodin, Hobbes and Rousseau, and implicitly of Hegel and National Socialism, Facism and Communism.

12. Text in Preston, Ronald H. ed. Technology and Social Justice. An International Symposium on the Social and Economic Teaching of the World Council of Churches from Geneva to Uppsala 1968. Valley Forge: Judson Press, 1971.

13. "If you substitute the phrase 'public interest' for 'common good'. you have a topic that ... preoccupies many American political scientists." Dahl, Robert A., "Political Theory: Truth and Consequences", in Readings in Modern Political Analysis, edited by Robert A. Dahl and Deane E. Neubuer. Englewood Cliffs: Prentice-Hall, 1968. p. 59.

14. Maritain. op. cit., pp. 11-12.

15. Cf., e.g., deJouvenal, Betrand. Sovreignty: An Inquiry into the Political Good. Translated by J. F. Huntington. Chicago: University of Chicago Press, 1957. p. 42, "fixity in environment"; and also Murray, John Courtney, Commentary on the "Declaration on Religious Freedom", in The Documents of Vatican II. New York: Guild Press, 1966. p. 686, ftnt. 20.

16. Gallup, George H. The Gallup Poll. Public Opinion, 1935-71. New York: Random House, 1972. Hereafter cited as The Gallup Poll. p. 1935.

17. Gallup, George, Jr., "The Public Opinion Referendum", in Public Opinion Quarterly. XXXV:2. (Summer, 1971) p. 226.

18. Gallup, George H. The Gallup Poll, Public Opinion, 1972-1978. Wilmington, Delaware: Scholarly Resources, Inc., 1970. pp. 582, 584.

19. The Gallup Poll, p. 1863.

20. Ogren, Evelyn H., "Public Opinions about Public Welfare", in Social Work. Vol. 18:1. (June, 1973). p. 104.

21. Although religion had been seen as losing influence in American life during the '60's (in 1970, 75% felt that religion was losing its influence on American life, The Gallup Poll, p. 2240), current public opinion seems evenly divided: in 1976, 44% believe religion is increasing its influence, while 45% believe it is losing influence. (Gallup Poll, Public Opinion 1972-1977. p. 931).

Interesting cross-cultural comparisons are also in evidence. In England, in 1957, Gallup found an intriguing response to this question: "What would you say has more influence on the way people live and their circumstances -- religion or politics?"
    Response: Politics -- 41%;
               Religion -- 30%
               About the same -- 17%.
(The Gallup Poll. p. 1482.)

More recently, 1978, 53% of Canadians thought religion was losing its influence while only 26% thought its influence was increasing. (Gallup, George H. The International Gallup Polls. Public Opinion, 1978. Wilmington, Delaware: Scholarly Resources, Inc., 1980.) Canadian opinion is in some contrast to that of their American neighbors.

22. Williams, Robin M., Jr. op. cit. p. 269.

23. Lenski, Gerhard. The Religious Factor. Garden City: Doubleday Anchor, 1963. p. 206.

24. Wilson, Bryan. _Religion_ _in_ _Secular_ _Society_.
    Baltimore: Penguin, 1969. p. 80.

25. But cf. Glock, Charles Y. and Stark, Rodney.
    Religion _and_ _Society_ _in_ _Tension_. Chicago:
    Rand McNally, 1965. Chapters 10 and 11.

26. Williams, Robin M. Jr., op. cit. p. 170.

27. Ibid., p. 176. Italics added.

28. Sutton, Francis X et al. _The_ _American_
    Business _Creed_. Cambridge: Harvard University
    Press, 1956. pp. 19-20.

29. Mr. Tyre Taylor, General Counsel of the
    Southern States Industrial Council, testifying
    before the Senate Committee on Currency and
    Banking, August, 1949. Quoted in (and fuller
    statement on) pp. 28-29 of Sutton et al. op. cit.

30. Bower, Howard R. in _Christian_ _Values_ _and_
    Economic _Life_, by John C. Bennett et al.
    N. Y.: Harper and Bros., 1954. p. 75.

31. Blough, Roy, "World Economic Policy and Planning:
    An American Perspective", in Denys Munby, ed.
    Economic _Growth_ _in_ _World_ _Perspective_. New York:
    Association Press, 1966. p. 252.

32. Boorstin, Daniel. _The_ _Decline_ _of_ _Radicalism_.
    New York: Random House, 1969. p. 35.

33. Sutton et al. op. cit. p. 19.

34. Cf. Glover, John D. _The_ _Attack_ _on_ _Big_
    Business. Boston: Harvard University, Division
    of Research, Graduate School of Business
    Administration, 1954.

35. Blau, Peter M. and Duncan, Otis Dudley. _The_
    American _Occupational_ _Structure_. New York:
    John Wiley and Sons, Inc., 1967. p. 278.

36. Hanser, Philip M., "Labor Force", in Robert E. L. Faris, Handbook of Modern Sociology. Chicago: Rand McNally & Co., 1964. p. 182.

37. Ibid.

38. Beale, Calvin L. et al. Characteristics of the U.S. Population by Farm and Nonfarm Origins. Washington, D.C.: Agricultural Economic Report, No. 66. U.S. Department of Agriculture, Economic Research Series, December, 1964. The sample was in excess of 25 million. Table on p. 6.

39. Ibid., p. 11.

40. Beale et al., op. cit. Data on pages 6 and 11

41. Blau and Duncan, op. cit. p. 102.

42. Op. cit. p. 41.

43. Op. cit. Chart, p. 102.

44. Williams, Robin M., Jr. op. cit. p. 176.

45. Samuelsson, Kurt. Religion and Economic Activity. London: Heinemann, 1961. p. 47. Although Samuelsson's general thesis is to disprove Weber, his analysis here does not depend on the cogency of that dispute about the Protestant ethic.

46. For data about England, cf. Laslett, Peter. The World We Have Lost. New York: Charles Scribners Sons, 1965. Chapter 4; and Laslett, Peter, ed. Household and Family in Past Time. London: Cambridge University Press, 1972, esp. Laslett's own monograph, "Mean Household Size in England Since the Sixteenth Century", pp. 125-158. Laslett maintains that multi-generational households never reached one in ten in pre-industrial England.

For America (particularly New England), see
Sidney M. Greenfield, "Industrialization and
the Family in Sociological Theory", The
American Journal of Sociology, Vol. 67:2
(1961). pp. 312-322.

47. Cf. Parsons, Talcott and Bales, R.F. Family,
Socialization and Interaction Process.
Glencoe: The Free Press, 1955. The authors
insist that now "we are dealing with a more
highly differentiated and specialized agency",
but one that has not failed.

48. Hansen, Paul G., "Family Relations and the
Behaviorial Sciences", in Oscar E. Feucht,
ed. Family Relationships and the Church.
St. Louis, Mo.: Concordia Publishing House,
1970. p. 181.

49. A perceptive student in a class I was conducting
exclaimed: "The family doesn't do any of those
things!"

50. Parsons, op. cit. pp. 16-17.

51. Scherer, Ross, "The American Family in the
Midst of Change", in Feucht, Family Relationships
and the Church, op. cit. p. 139.

52. Elmer, M. C. Sociology of the Family. Boston:
Ginn & Co., 1945. pp. 227-228.

53. Hansen, Paul G. art. cit. p. 177.

54. Burgess, E. The Family: From Institution
to Companionship. New York: American Book
Company, 1945. p. 26.

55. Cf. ibid. Also Cavan, Routh Shoule. The
American Family. 3rd ed. New York: Thomas
Crowell Co., 1963; and Green, Arnold W.,
"The Middle Class Male Child and Neurosis",
in American Sociological Review, XI. (Feb.
1946) pp. 31-41.

56. Mariante, Benjamin R. and Seymour, Linda, "The Anomic Middle Years of Marriage". Unpublished research report. University of San Francisco, 1967.

57. Stephens, William N., "Family and Kinship", in Neil J. Smelser, ed. _Sociology_. New York: John Wiley, 1967. p. 539.

58. How it got outside the "sacred canopy" is another question. It was probably the last social institution to withdraw, and more by default as all the other institutions had pulled out. As religion became privatized, so has the family.

59. Luckmann, op. cit. p. 6. Cf. also, Inkeles, Alex. _What Is Sociology?_ Englewood Cliffs: Prentice Hall, 1964. p. 68; and Lundberg, Geroge A. et. al. _Sociology_. 4th edition. New York: Harper and Row, 1968. p. 709.

63

CHAPTER 3

SOCIO-CULTURAL PLURALISM:
ANALYSIS AND INTERPRETATION.

We have seen that there is evidence for another process that is part of that complex of processes that has been called "modernization". Besides urbanization, industrialization and bureaucratization,[1] this other process, the establishment of autonomous institutions, has occurred. This process has been called pluralization, and the "pluralistic modern situation" is as good a shorthand description as any.

The evidence that is available to establish the existence of pluralism is more than suggestive. While evidence of this kind can rarely be "conclusive" in the finalistic way that an opinion or preference poll is, or much less, the establishment of a physical law, it is certainly as strong as that for other processes of social change or value orientation that are regularly accepted by social scientists as data to be examined and interpreted. Moreover those few social scientists that have turned their attention to this situation acknowledge the existence of socio-cultural pluralism and in fact try to offer an interpretation of the "pluralistic modern situation". What I have done so far is simply to provide some documentation and precision to what "everyone already knows". At any rate, the evidence available is as good as any to see that what has arisen as part of the modern world are a number of self-sufficient institutions, depending on their own rationale and own first principles for justification and legitimation in the working, everyday world. They do not and need not look beyond themselves. The development of institutions of this kind is "pluralization".

DEFINITIONS

There are several descriptive definitions of pluralism, and it is perhaps profitable at this point to draw some of these definitions together. In the article on "Pluralism" in <u>Scaramentum Mundi</u>, Hättich describes pluralism in this way for a theological audience:

> In this strict sense, this is the division of society into numerous groups with varying interests, each of which considers itself equal to the others . . . A society with such structures cannot be represented by a series of concentric circles as if it were built up into a whole by the integration of each unit into a larger one. Group pluralism should be rather represented by a number of intersecting circles, arranged unsystematically and mobile in character. And overlapping occurs within the individual himself.[2]

Peter Berger and Thomas Luckmann, who perhaps more than any other sociologists have analyzed pluralism, use this definition:

> We would define pluralism as a situation in where there is competition in the institutional ordering of comprehensive meanings for everyday life. Historically such competition generally succeeds a situation in which it was more or less absent. That is, pluralism is the consequence of a historical process of de-monopolization.[3]

Andrew Greeley, the director for the NORC Study of Pluralism, uses a very broad description of pluralism. He writes:

> By pluralism, I mean a situation in which society must balance not merely different social class groups but also

different geographic, racial, religious and nationality groups.[4]

Finally, J. Milton Yinger in assessing the relationship between pluralism and religion and secularization offers this definition:

> I shall use it in the most general sense to refer to a situation in which a society is divided into subsocieties with distinct cultural traditions. Pluralism is thus one form of social differentiation. It can be distinguished from the universal variety based on differentiation of role by the fact that pluralistic differences are related to separate social structures and cultural systems.[5]

These wide-ranging conceptualizations of pluralism indicate the divergent but overlapping areas that have been scrutinized by sociologists and theologians. The data that I have presented in the preceding chapter indicates what elements from among these definitions can be documented for my purposes and provide as well the elements that are relevant to the contemporary religio-social situation.[6]

What the evidence shows is that a variety of intersecting world-views co-exist in the modern world, each world-view legitimating a certain segment of the social world and often competing to dominate the legitimating process in a broader realm. This data specifically applies to institutional structures and their attempts at self-legitimation. Other more tenuous social structures, forces and institutions undoubtedly must be recognized in this process; e.g., Berger mentions "modern value systems of 'individualism' or sexual emanicipation",[7] to which could be added a host of others, such as "return to nature", cultural hedonism, anti-establishmentarianism and so on.

67

However, this data suggests that pluralism can be documented for a cluster of sociological institutions that have become clearly differentiated in modern, specifically American society. What is unique about the present socio-cultural situation is the degree of differentiation and the relatively complete "autonomization" of these universally present institutions.

I would like to describe pluralism as the varied and various ways in which the meaning of everyday life is integrated and structured. This varied structuring has two dimensions, subjective or personal, and social or institutionalized in society. These two dimensions are interrelated in that the personal and the institutional are generallly considered to have a high degree of correlation.

(It should be noted that pluralism describes a situation in which a minimum core interpretation of the universe is shared and taken for granted. This interpretation can derive mainly from content, or from context, or even, as was noted before, from agreement about process.)

Now when the structuring of the meaning of life is extended to interpret the entire cosmos and is given symbolic form and integrative function, it is usually called religion (although it may be a para-religious symbolization or a religious surrogate). But we have seen that there is a lack of overall legitimation of the forms, processes and directions of the plurality of world-views as they assume symbolic and institutionalized form in the post-industrial world.

One further point should be noted in connection with this description of pluralism. Because we will consider the subjective or social psychological dimensions of pluralism in correlation with the societal or "objective", we can consider "institutions" to refer both to patterned ways of doing things as well as agencies through which major aspects of society are cared for. Thus "work" can be considered as a kind of behavior, the pattern in our society by which an individual supports himself and his dependents; or as the economic agency that is there for individuals to enter into to satisfy economic needs. Both aspects of the institutions have been "pluralized".

The consequences of socio-cultural pluralism will be examined in subsequent sections of this chapter. But first a brief distinction must be made between this new kind of pluralism and the earlier ethnic pluralism of the age of immigration to the United States.

ETHNIC AND RELIGIOUS PLURALISM

An earlier form of pluralism dominated industrialized American culture (i.e., outside the South) for several decades; this was the pluralism of the ethnic migrants. The experience of millions of "uprooted" led to the formation of socio-cultural groups based on national origin or identity. Oscar Handlin describes this process in The Uprooted:

> At many steps in his life's journey he (the migrant) came to points beyond which he could not go on along... Consequently the newcomers took pains early to seek out those whom experience made their brothers; and to organize each other's support, they created a great variety of formal and informal institutions.[8]

Handlin then goes on to describe some of these "informal institutions" which are clearly voluntary institutions, albeit of a special import for their membership. Informal gatherings, he hypothesizes, led to institutions for funeral insurance and other insurance and to mutual aid associations. Schools for some, especially Irish Catholics, came into existence, a score of language newspapers and even a developed and sophisticated ethnic theater, especially among Jews from eastern Europe, arose for the preservation of a socio-cultural heritage.

But all of this was -- and still is where it exists today[9] -- a different kind of pluralism, columnar rather than overlapping. The entire world-view for each ethnic group was (is) supported and rationalized by those not only of like mind but also of like culture who form institutions to sustain this world-view. Everything had a place in the old world, and new institutions are formed precisely to give this sense of security and of a well-ordered cosmos for the uprooted in the new world. The existence of many groups who had their own integrated cosmos comprised ethnic pluralism.

Neither was the formation of voluntary associations a new social phenomenon. Admission to these associations was based on national-cultural origins and adherence was determined by willingness to preserve something of the old norms and institutions to guarantee the legitimation of a sacred cosmos.

In this way ethnic pluralism does not differ greatly from religious pluralism. The denomination (and the sect) is a voluntary association that has certain conditions for admissions and adherence, e.g., baptism and acceptance of the basic tenets of the denomination, an implied view of outsiders as different if not inferior, etc.

From the perspective we are focusing on here, the purpose of the denomination and the sect is to give order and meaning in a specifically religious way to the social world as a whole. And as such, theoretically it does not admit of pluralism, although it exists almost by definition in an incipient pluralistic situation.

These have been specific kinds of pluralism in the American situation and certainly legitimate areas for investigation. However, they are not what I consider to be the specifically new socio-cultural phenomenon of pluralism. Possibly they belong to the period in religious and social "evolution" that Bellah would call "early modern".[10]

In fact, ethnic and religious pluralism have been assimilated into the broader pluralistic situation and must compete with other institutions in the modern world. "Old fashioned (ethnic) political communities and religious communities themselves now become only two among many new, but once unimagined, fellowships."[11]

THE CONSEQUENCES OF PLURALISM

The pluralistic situation in which we now find ourselves presents competing institutionalized patterns which form the values and behavior patterns not in a totally integrated way for the whole of life but merely for the operation and smooth self-serving function of that institution alone. The effects of this have been far-reaching but as yet not specifically explored. I will examine three that have special implications for a consideration of the Church.

The first and most noticeable consequence has been the relativizing of values and norms. The value system of each institution, group or association, while applicable and normative chiefly for that institution is not readily transferable to extra-institutional situations.

A second consequence which has been obvious to many but not specifically related to the pluralistic situation is the fragmentation or segmentation of modern society. Each institution or association pre-cisely because it has been able to specialize, es-tablish its own norms and devise its own patterns of values, has set up an autonomous and self-sus-taining system. The result of this has been that each area of modern life has been set apart from other areas, not only because of a separation of work

71

and home, but more profoundly because of the relative autonomy of each social sector. This segmentation has become the model that all institutions seek to emulate.

The third consequence, following upon this and of concern for this consideration, is the changed place of religion in this pluralistic context. Religion as the individual's own belief and value system or as an integrative and supportative institution in the social fabric no longer enjoys the monopoly of legitimating and giving meaning to the individual or social worlds. In fact, no institution seems able to claim such a monopoly now. As Berger and Luckmann point out:

> Pluralism entails the transformation of religious institutions from primary to secondary ones, that is, from contrasting monopolistic institutions of the public sphere to voluntary, competitive institutions of private life. The religious institutions are now not only in competition with each other, but with the other meaning-and-identity supplying agencies available on the market.[12]

We will consider each of these consequences in more depth presently. First, however, it is important to consider briefly the socio-psychological implications of a pluralistic world.

Pluralism of Consciousness

> It is not that a single world has replaced a double one but that an infinitely multiplex one has replaced the simple duplex structure (of historical religion). It is not that life has become again a "one possibility thing" but that it has become an infinite possibility thing.[13]

It is this multiplex world in which the individual now finds himself and indeed, "The

72

kind of 'world' which the individual creates
is one which is largely tied to the multiple,
everyday realities of an industrial society."[14]

A perceptive analysis of multiple realities
is provided by Alfred Schutz, although Schutz'
principle interest is on the various levels of
reality as they inhere in the consciousness of
each individual, e.g., dreams, fantasy, everyday world, etc. However, his analysis can be
applied to vertical dimensions of multiple reality
as well as to the above-mentioned horizontal
levels.

Schutz describes "multiple realities" in
terms of the interest or tension they produce.
In this analysis, working reality or the everyday world is that which has the most interest for
normal people. This reality, however, is not
out of nowhere. Although Schutz does not pursue
this aspect of his analysis, the working world
is always an intersubjective world, and the
world that is the working area of interests and
tensions is a world of many structures, or institutionalized normative interactions in a "multiplex" arena. It is these many interactions in
many institutions that make for the "multiple
realities" of the everyday working world of the
normal individual. Schutz himself quotes approvingly
and correlates his presentation with that of
William James, citing the various "sub-universes"
that James analyzes as part of the consciousness
of human experience. James concludes:

> Each world whilst it is attended to is
> real after its own fashion; only the reality
> lapses with the tension.[15]

It is this interest and attention that places
the individual in one of these "multiple realities",
one of the "sub-universes" of the autonomous and
self-legitimating institutions of the pluralistic,
modern world. What has happened in the field of
social realities, from the participants' point

of view, is that for the working self in the field
of wide-awakeness the area of social relevance
is itself multiple. What obtains is a situation
in which the real for each area of social interaction becomes self-contained. The "real" from
among the "multiple realities" establishes its
own reality for its own participants. The
"sacred canopy" is dissolved for the working,
everyday world of modern man.

RELATIVIZING OF VALUES

It is the dissolution of an over-arching,
legitimating system that has led as well to the
development of a multiplex value system. Each
social institution, in providing its own first
principles, includes among these its own set of
priorities and thus implicitly if not explicitly
a set of values. For the individual, the difficulty is to distinguish different sets of values
and the struggle to let go when they are no longer
applicable in terms of a different institution
in a multiplex world.

On the societal scale, "the universe of values
is intractably pluralistic."[16] Williams states in
an earlier consideration, "(modern) societies may
be characterized by value distributions, and by
the arrangement of subsystems of values in
different portions of the social structure."[17]

This great complexity of interacting institutions and perforce of their value systems leads
to a general relativizing of these systems, both
in the sense that one may very well be as "good
or as relevant" as another and in the sense that
the institutionalization of a plurality of
world-views is simply the modern version of the
problem of Heraclitus, the sceptics, and meta-
physicians: what is the nature of the really
real?

Berger sums up the situation succinctly from
the sociology of knowledge perspective:

74

> The theologians' world has become
> one world among many -- A generalization
> of the problem of relativity ... To put
> it simply: History points to the pro-
> blem of relativity as a fact, the socio-
> logy of knowledge as a necessity of our
> condition."[18]

SEGMENTATION

The segmentation of modern society resulted
from the universal complexity of social, political
and economic systems. This fragmentation into
separate, quasi-air-tight compartments is an
inevitable result of the universal specialization,
expertise and professionalism required in every
sector of modern society. Once again, however,
we can perceive this to be a function of the
development of a pluralistic situation. The world
of multiple realities is bound to give rise to
a variety of specialized functions, values and
world-views.

What happens with this kind of specialization
is differentiation: differentiation of task or
function, of institution and of organization.
Thus, the development of a host of separate and
autonomous institutional patterns and organizations
in every field is the result of the process of
pluralization. Each of the major institutional
systems -- economic, politics, family, and religion
-- develops a whole sub-set of institutions imbued
with and governed by the world view, values and
principles that have been developed in these major
components of society.

As Parsons has pointed out, it is this socio-
cultural process of differentiation that has
subtracted the tasks from institutional religion
in a movement "from fusions of religious and non-
religious components in the same action structures
to increasingly clear differentiation between
multiple spheres of action."[19] It is these

multiple spheres of action, a multiplex world, a pluralistic world that has developed, making a religion a secondary, rather than a primary, institution in modern society.

LOSS OF MONOPOLISTIC CONTROL

A third consequence of the development of pluralism is the loss of a monopoly on world-views on the part of institutionalized religion. This is something more than the ecclesial loss of monopoly in the rise of denominationalism. This latter was the struggle over which particular world-view was to provide the total value system for society; but there was no dispute about the place of the religious institution: all agreed that religion was to provide the ordering and valency of values; the only dispute was which religious form of institutionalization was to provide the world-view and concomitant value structure.

This is very much changed now. As Berger and Luckmann have pointed out in the paragraph already quoted, religious institutions are no longer the only "meaning-and-identity-supplying agencies available on the market".[20] In fact, in a world where there are multiple spheres of action, no one institutional sphere is capable of monopolistic imposition of a meaning-and-value system. Rather, as Bellah, insists, the possibility now exists for an infinitely multiplex construction of meaning, value and order in modern society.

This will tend to lower the level of commitment but it does provide the possibility of a more diversified society:

It is becomming rare to value any belief more than life. To be willing to die for a belief means to be unable to conceive of an acceptable life outside the framework of that belief. The pluralistic and hetergeneous quality of

76

present-day experience undermines such
exclusive beliefs.[21]

This may simply mean, however, that no
individual is so wrapped up in one value system
that it becomes a monomaniacal concern. In a
pluralistic situation the possibility surely exists
for real dedication when the focus of interest
and tension is high in one phase of everyday world;
but the pull from the multiple realities of everyday existence temper the commitment, not attempting
to smother it but providing a balance to prevent
its take-over of any personality. The monopoly
has been broken.

At any rate, no one institution can claim to
offer a monopoly on sanctioning the order and
process of the universe. There are instead many
views overlapping and interacting in the individual
personality, and indeed in the institutional
structure of modern society.

THE EFFECTS ON RELIGION

With the development of pluralism which
includes the autonomy of individual institutions,
what has been the effects on religion as an
institution? Has religion become privatized;
or more specialized; or reduced to a small minority
of adherents?

Salisbury's judgment, that "it is quite possible
that there is neither more religion nor less
religion than there used to be in American society,
but rather religion is more diffused and less
intense,"[22] gives us an indication of the direction
of religion and a clue to what has happened.
The prevalence of religion per se in the individual's
life may be no less pervasive if less intense;
but there has been a real change in the institutional significance of religion; and this is my
central concern.

77

For most of the population, religious institutions, loosely, "The Churches", have passed
from the stage of primary institutions to
secondary institutions. The "Churches" are no
longer mandatory; they are voluntary associations
not on the model of the voluntary free churches
which arose in a society where it was presumed
that you belonged to some church, denomination
or sect (although as we shall see, there are
certain theological elements of the free church
that suit religious institutions now). Rather
in the contemporary scene there is no such
presumption of church membership. The "Churches"
themselves must compete not only with each other
on the "market model" proposed in the early 1960's
by Peter Berger[23] but with other institutions as
the supportative, integrative, and evaluative institutions. Bryan Wilson suggests that aesthetics
will take over from religion[24] but I suggest that
anything can take over these functions of religion
that can provide a sense of transcendence for any
given individual in modern society. This is the
condition of the infinitely multiplex world in
which individuals find themselves.

Thus, a distinction analogous to Cooley's
distinction of primary and secondary groups can
be made between primary and secondary institutions.
Religious institutions (if not religion itself)
have passed from the status of being primary to
functioning as secondary institutions in our
society. Thus, instead of being a general, spontaneous and more-or-less all-encompassing
institutions, it is specialized, limited and
constraining within its own sphere of efficacy.[25]
It is no longer expected that every inidividual
in our society will be a member of a religious
institution, nor is "religion" ascribed or
"inherited"; rather individuals seem to change
denominations with some frequency or to drop
out, at least for a time, from the religious scene
altogether. Finally, as Luckmann makes clear,

> The continuous dependence of the
> secondary institutions on consumer pre-

ference and, thus, on the "private sphere"
makes it very unlikely that the social
objectivation of themes originating in
the "private sphere" and catering to it
will eventually lead to the articulation
of a consistent and closed sacred cosmos
and the specialization, once again, of
religious institutions. This is one of
the several reasons that justify the
assumption that we are not merely describing
an interregnum between the extinction of
one "official" model and the appearance
of a new one, but rather, that we are
observing the emergence of a new social
form of religion.26

SECULARIZATION AND PLURALISM

The evidence and the direction of this line
of thought might seem to be leading along the
familiar lines that attempt to establish the
process of secularization in modern society.
Berger and Luckmann believed that secularization
and pluralism are twin phenomena in the modern
social order (although Luckmann seems to have
later changed his mind). This view may turn out
to be correct; but it is possible that secularization
and pluralism are somewhat different explanations
for the same social process and societal events.
As with all sociological explanations, the question
is not only which interpretation gives the best
explanation and understanding of events, (for
both may be correct), but also which explanation
best explains "social facts" from a particular
viewpoint or with a particular problem in mind.
Finally, in line with the thinking of some of the
"founding fathers" of sociology as well as some
of the contemporary "radical" sociologists, which
explanation will help us ameliorate social conditions
and create more responsive social institutions,
in this case, religious or ecclesial institutions,
and even religion itself? Secularization may be
a good enough diagnostic explanation; but pluralism,
it seems to me, gives a better prognosis.

Usually sociologists of religion as well as theologians trace the cognitive roots of secularization to the Bible where they believe they see evidence of the "disenchantment of the world" in the various Yahwist commands that established the seculum or world as its own distinct sphere, separated from "the gods". But it is precisely when the various elements or institutions of the world, the seculum, become their own sphere that they can become autonomous, have their own raison d'etre and work out their own responsibilities. This does not deny that any of these theatres are immune to God's activity (or the invasion of the transcendent), but simply that they have their own narrow but self-contained domain. Social institutions in this Biblical view are freed to be themselves, as the "secular theologians" maintain; but autonomy of institutions implies more not less responsibility, as it does of individuals. The pluralistic explanation may provide a better explanation (as well as prognosis) than the secularization explanation.

Sociologically as well as cognitively pluralism might offer a more comprehensive explanation of what has occurred in the modern institutional order. As the social structure in a scientific and technologically expanding society has become more complex demanding the development of segmented, specialized institutions, these institutions developed their own responses and in fact developed into total systems to meet the social needs confronting a complexifying society. It is possible to describe this as a process of secularization in which, as the traditional explanation goes, social institutions, especially the polity and the economy, moved out from under the sanctioning and justifying religious system. But it is also possible to explain the process as one of developing institutional pluralism. Just as previous various ethnic groups or denominations set up quasi-self-contained worlds, with their own value systems and justifications, so here a similar process, even more comprehensive, develops within these major or primary institutions in modern society.

The chief difference between this and an older pluralism that must be pointed out is that these institutions make no special claim to provide ultimate significance or the central core of meaning either to society as a whole or to any individuals who participate in these institutions. This is one of the distinctive traits of modern pluralism, which, as we shall see, provides a special opportunity for religion in the modern world. As Andrew Greeley remarks:

> The important question for religion is not whether it continues to play a role in human life, but whether it can provide man values which are relevant not only in its particular institutional sphere, but in all the other institutional spheres -- the political, the economic, the international, which impinge on his consciousness.[27]

Pluralism not only may provide a better prognosis for some kind of institutional religion than secularization; it may also provide a better explanation for the data that have been assembled, and in fact may explain secularization itself. Greeley, in Religion in the Year 2000, summarizes a great deal of data from various studies to show that secularization is not occurring, or at least is occurring at a nearly imperceptible rate. "As far as (American) Gentiles are concerned then, secularization, if it is occurring at all, is occurring at so slow a rate that no measure of it could be found in the thirteen years (1952-1965) covered by the two studies."[28] What should be noted about the evidence that Greeley summarizes, in a chapter of some 40 pages, is the institutional context of the material. In the context of the religious institution, people will respond in a religious way -- they will be 96% religious; but will they be "secular" in the context of other institutions? What I believe the full evidence suggests is not that people will be either "religious" or "secular", but that they will be "economic", or "political" or "recreational", or

"religious", depending on the institutional
context implied in the questions that are asked.
Bellah is right; it is a multiplex world, not
dualistic -- good vs. evil, sacred vs. secular.
Yet it is precisely the intellectual baggage of
dualism -- perhaps as cultural lag, perhaps as
underground Manicheism -- that has infected and
prevented true insight; and this has led to the
present impasse. But an attempt to formulate
a view of socio-cultural pluralism is an effort to
move beyond this dualism, and to analyze social
reality from a different viewpoint, one which
perhaps gives a picture closer to the reality we
experience.

    This line of analysis can be pursued even
further. Berger states that "the phenomenon
called 'pluralism' is a social-structural correlate
of the secularization of consciousness."[29] But
is this putting the cart before the horse? Is it
a change in consciousness, a social psychological
alteration that is primary; or is it a social
structural alteration that takes precedence?
While granting that the two are never independent
of each other, it does seem more accurate,
historically and sociologically,[30] to attribute
the primary change to the socio-institutional
order which became "secularized", i.e., autonomous
from an overarching and integrating sacred cosmos.
In this light it might be as accurate to say,
"Secularization occurred and brought about a plural
allegiance of consciousness." It depends on what
is designated as secularized, the social structural
or the social psychological; and what is designated
as pluralized.

    My contention in this sociological analysis
has been simply that a fresh examination of the
evidence can be adequately interpreted by a theory
of pluralism. This can explain "secularization"
on the institutional level and still account for
the data that Greeley and NORC can accumulate.
In fact, it provides a common root for both sets
of data, and thus seems more adequate because it

is more comprehensive and can account for the inconsistencies.

We have seen that institutions themselves have become autonomous in the modern world, and this is how secularization is usually described. "By secularization we mean the process by which sectors of society and culture are removed from the domination of religious institutions and symbols."[31] But this process, as we have seen is somewhat more complicated, and certainly should not be viewed solely in a negative way -- as removal; it is rather the process of establishing an independent institution with its own first principles and raison d'etre.

Now when the world of religious institutions becomes the focus of the individual's consciousness in terms of his everyday experience, he is going to live, respond and act in that world. And about 96% of Americans respond positively in that institutional context, when this is the focus of consciousness. (An individual may reject the world of religious institutions, much as some individuals of the "counter-culture" reject the techno-economic world we live in. For such individuals, these respective "worlds" have no meaning and responses to items on a questionnaire or an interview which reflect the appropriate institutional context would reflect this.) Most individuals are willing to accept the religious institutional pattern in society as part of the real world, much as they accept the economic institution. Thus their responses will be to these institutions as separate, autonomous institutions, i.e., their responses will be in the pluralistic framework. What has occurred is pluralization not secularization; people are religious when religion is at the center of conscious life, as on a questionnaire, "Do you believe in God?" They are economic when the economy is at the center, as on a questionnaire, "What is the most important problem facing America today?" The largest response now will have to do with the economy, although a few years ago it would have concerned the Indo-China War.

THE CHALLENGE

My emphasis on a socio-cultural theory of pluralism is more than an academic exercise. As I indicated at the beginning of this chapter, I believe it is the neglected dimension of the process we call "modernization", and unlike the other dimensions of urbanization, bureaucratization, and industrialization, we haven't sufficiently investigated "the global dynamics of pluralism as a phenomenon grounded in the infrastructures of modern societies."[32]

The limited issue that I wish to face in the second part of this monograph is the future of the "Church", or instititutional forms of religion. If the "sacred canopy" no longer gives institutional sanction and meaning, is there an ecclesiology that can face this modern condition and provide a form and function for a church in our multiplex and pluralistic universe?

REFERENCES

1. Cf. Worsley, Peter et.al. Introducing
   Sociology. Baltimore, Md.: Penquin Books,
   1970. p. 269, and Stein, M. Eclipse
   of Community. Princeton: Princeton University
   Press, 1960. pp. 5, 55, 107 and passim.

2. Hättich, Manfred, "Pluralism", in Sacramentum
   Mundi, Vol. V. New York: Herder & Herder,
   1970. p. 33.

3. Berger, Peter, and Luckmann, Thomas,
   "Secularization and Pluralism", in
   International Yearbook for the Sociology of
   Religion. Vol. II. Koln: Westdeutscher,
   Verlag, 1966. p. 73.

4. Greeley, Andrew M. The Denominational
   Society. Glennview, Ill.: Scott, Foresman
   and Company, 1972. p. 116.

5. Yinger, J. Milton, "Pluralism, Religion and
   Secularism", in Journal for the Scientific
   Study of Religion, Vol. VI, No. 1
   (Spring, 1967). pp. 17-18.

6. This doesn't imply that other "variables"
   cannot be documented, only that these seemed
   sufficient for my present purposes.

7. Berger, Peter. The Sacred Canopy. New York:
   Doubleday Anchor Books, 1967. p. 137.

8. Handlin, Oscar O. The Uprooted. Boston:
   Little, Brown & Co., 1952. p. 170.

9. Cf. Greeley, Andrew, Why Can't They Be Like
   Us? America's White Ethnic Groups. New York:
   Dutton, 1971 and Novak, Michael, The Rise
   of the Unmeltable Ethnics. New York:
   MacMillan, 1972.

85

10. Cf. Bellah, R. L. "Religious Evolution", in American Sociological Review, Vol. 29, No. 3 (June, 1964). p. 368. This article is widely anthologized and also appears in Bellah's collected essays, Beyond Belief Essays on Religion in a Post-Traditional World. New York: Harper & Row, 1970.

11. Boorstin, Daniel J. The Decline of Radicalism. New York: Random House, 1969. p. 39.

12. Berger and Luckmann, "Secularization and Pluralism," art. cit., cited in ftnt 3.

13. Bellah, R. N., art. cit., p. 371. Bellah goes on to say: "The analysis of modern man as secular, materialistic, dehumanized and in the deepest sense areligious seems to me fundamentally misguided, for such a judgment is based on standards that cannot adequately gauge the modern temper."

14. Robertson, Roland. The Sociological Interpretation of Religion. New York: Schocken Books, 1970. p. 201.

15. In Schutz, Alfred. Collected Papers, Vol. I. "On Multiple Realities", The Hague: Martinus Nijhoff, 1971, p. 207 from James, William, Principles of Psychology, Vol. II, Chapter XXI.

16. Williams, Robin J., Jr., American Society, cited above Chap. 2. p. 500.

17. Williams, Robin M., Jr., "Individual and Group Values", p. 27 of The Annals, Vol. 371, (May, 1967). Italics added.

18. Berger, Peter. A Rumor of Angels. New York: Doubleday Anchor Books, 1970. p. 38.

19. Parsons, Talcot, "Christianity and Modern Industrial Society", in Tiryakian, Edward (ed.) _Sociological Theory, Values and Sociocultural Change. Essays in Honor of Pitirim A. Sorokin._ New York: The Free Press of Clencoe, 1963. p. 37.

20. Berger and Luckmann, _loc. cit._

21. Wheelis, Allen, "The Quest for Identity", in Rosenberg, Bernard (ed.) _Analysis of Contemporary Society_, I. New York: Thomas Y. Crowell Co., 1961. p. 21.

22. Salisbury, W. Seward. _Religion in American Culture._ Homewood, Ill.: Dorsey Press, 1964. p. 480.

23. Cf. Berger, Peter, "A Market Model for the Analysis of Ecumenicity", _Social Research_, 30:1. (Spring, 1963).

24. Cf. Wilson, Bryan. _Religion in Secular Society._ Baltimore: Penquin Books, 1969. esp. pp. 64-66.

25. Cf. Cooley, Charles Horton. _Human Nature and the Social Order._ Rev. ed. New York: Scribner's, 1922, and Davis, Kingsley. _Human Society._ New York; MacMillan, 1957. esp. p. 306.

26. Luckmann, T. _The Invisible Religion._ cited above. pp. 104-105.

27. Greeley, Andrew. _The Hesitant Pilgrim. American Catholicism After the Council._ New York: Image Books, 1969. p. 64.

28. Greeley, Andrew. _Religion in the Year 2000._ New York: Sheed and Ward, 1969. p. 36.

29. Berger, Peter. _The Sacred Canopy._ p. 127, cited above.

30. Cf. Luckmann, _op. cit._, and Boorstin, _op. cit._

31. Berger, _op_. _cit_., p. 107.

32. Berger, _op_. _cit_., p. 138.

PART III.

THEOLOGICAL APPLICATION.

PART III.

THEOLOGICAL APPLICATION.

CHAPTER 4

A THEOLOGY FOR A MULTIFORM CHURCH

In "discovering" the theological principles involved in the possibility, description and ecclesiology of a multiform or polystructured Church, I am not inventing a "new" theology of institutions. Rather, I intend to apply theological principles and positions to a pluralistic cultural situation; or perhaps at times, as George Tavard suggests, I shall be "pursuing a theological line of thought that could previously have remained unnoticed."1

In this discussion of an ecclesiology in the absence of a sacred canopy, let me briefly recapitulate the meaning of pluralism, especially with an eye to indicate its implications for a theology of the Church. Berger and Luckmann (in a passage already referred to) have succinctly described pluralism "as a situation in which there is competition in the institutional ordering of comprehensive meanings for everyday life."2 They add, significantly: "Historically such competition generally succeeds a situation in which it was more or less absent. That is pluralism is the consequence of a historical process of de-mono-polization."3 The possibility of this de-mono-polization and its effects on religion in modern society are what I have already considered. Here I want to consider: what theological principles can we discover or use that allow a Church to exist in a situation in which it no longer has a monopoly on the meaning-structures in our society?

There are two further ideas that should be clarified, especially in light of the discussion in the previous chapter. Berger and Luckmann, in further clarification, note: "it suffices to say that among the many socially recognized meanings

91

of everyday life there will always be some that
are comprehensive in the sense of supplying an
overall canopy for all the experiences of individual
existence."[4] While I tend to agree with this
statement, at least in regard to most individuals,
I believe it should be pointed out that for the
individual comprehensive meanings change at
different times during the course of his life and
in response to different critical periods in each
individual's biography. Moreover, Berger and
Luckmann are applying this qualification to the
"experience of individual existence". Modern
society may not have a single comprehensive meaning
system.

Milton Yinger adds a further clarification
that helps us to understand the impact of pluralism
both on the social structure and on the individual's
incorporation or internalization of the social
structure.

> Pluralism is thus one form of social
> differentiation. It can be distinguished
> from the universal variety based on differ-
> entiation by role by the fact that plural-
> istic differences are related to separate
> social structures and cultural systems;
> whereas role differences represent a
> division of function within a shared system
> and based on a common culture.[5]

Pluralism thus tends toward a differentiation of
socio-cultural systems, a "sub-culture" of
differentiation. For the individuals in these sub-
cultures, this means that role, and role performance
and role sets, take on not only different styles
but different meanings in each different cultural
setting. The individual's performance of roles
is less determined by the sacred cosmos, and
"'secular' norms develop in more or less autonomous
political and economic institutions."[6] Consequently
the pluralism that obtains in the modern American
social scene is not that kind of pluralism which
includes "sharply different ethnic and religious

collectivities that have few positive social
bonds across lines of cleavage, being held together
by economic links and political domination."[7]
Examples of this latter kind of pluralism might be
Canada, Belgium or Yugoslavia. Northern Ireland
is a case of the collapse of this kind of pluralism.[8]

Confronted with a pluralistic situation as
described by Berger and Luckmann[9] is there a theology
to deal with the rift in the "sacred canopy"?
Scriptural evidence leads to the conclusion that
the Church was multiple at the beginning. In a
pluralistic situation, institutional specialization
has led to competition, and the Church has become
one among many competing institutions.

Instead the Church is to be leaven, catalyst,
sign of holiness in the world, and not the support
of ideologies that might develop in competing
institutions. The Church has a responsibility to
a world that is, in this hypothesis, pluralistic,
and is to bring redemption not only to individuals
but human social arrangements. I take redemption
to include human institutions; and if human social
arrangements are pluralistic, the Church must
manage not only to enter this pluralistic society
but to develop a theological understanding of her
relationship to such a society. In this view of
redemption, the world, individuals and institutions,
needs the Church, which means a Church willing to
meet the world.

Finally the rights of individuals to a multi-
form Church seem central to the Christian experience.
William Barrett makes this clear in his discussion
of freedom and order in the Church:

> Since the social good of Christians is
> diversified in kind and pluralistic in
> structure according to individual needs and
> aspirations, the right of free association,
> pluriformity in living the Christian
> experience, and the integrity of individual
> response to grace are primary values. Self-
> responsibility and self-determination are

radical Christian rights. The rights
and duties of authority, though more comprehensive, coexist within a galaxy of the
equally elemental rights of individuals
in themselves and in community.[10]

For individuals and for institutions, a multiform
Church seems to be theologically necessary.

The issue of pluriformity in the Church is a
problem first of all for a Catholic (and Catholic)
Christianity. Is it possible for the Christian
oekumene to come to grips with a pluralistic world
without losing itself? This question has certainly
arisen from the American religious experience
where the "main line" denominations had to face
the situation of religious pluralism. However
socio-cultural pluralism would appear to be a
quantum leap for the Christian churches and as
such poses a catholic problem. While here the
theology for a multiform Church will be drawn
from several traditions, several Catholic authors
will be utilized because they perhaps more than
others have had to face up to the problem of pluralism
earlier; but they are not the only ones to have
done so. And now it seems that the several
Christian traditions may have to focus on this
issue if the contention of Berger and Luckmann
is correct.

A CURRENT VIEW IN ECCLESIOLOGY

An aspect of ecclesiology that underlies much
of the current discussion about the Church,
especially in its relationship with the world as
a social order, is the stress on the blurred or
fluid boundaries between the Church and the world.
While this originally may have developed from a
heavy emphasis (over-emphasis?) on an Incarnational
Theology, this perspective, as we shall see, is
common currency among various emphases in ecclesiology on the contemporary scene. I will examine
this development in ecclesiology, that the

94

boundaries between Church and humanity are not
hard and fast, but flexible and fluid, and in
following sections extend this analysis to
specific theological currents.

This relationship between Church and human
world is derived from both the Incarnational and
Eschatological aspects of Christ's person and work.
First, the Incarnation means the taking on of
humanity on the part of the Logos. The Logos,
Christ, continues his presence as the source of
power and freedom in the Church and in a kind of
"mystical" identification with the Church. But
the Incarnation means not only fellowship with the
Church; primarily it means fellowship with all of
mankind. "Because of Christ's fellowship with us
(in the Church) the universal human fellowship,
too, takes on a deepened meaning, and the boundaries
between mankind and the Church begin to blur."[11]
The fellowship of the Logos with all of humanity
has given a new direction to the theology of the
Church.

Traditionally this Incarnational aspect of
ecclesiology has been developed -- and rightly so --
to maintain that members of the Church must
exemplify the meaning of grace or redemption.[12]
But beyond this call or vocation for the Christian
people as individuals, there is the mandate for
the Church as a whole. The Church must reveal in
exemplary fashion in its own institutional
patterns the reality and depth of redemption.

However, if this sign of redemption or freedom
is exemplary, it must be exemplary in terms of the
world -- of the social milieu in which the Church
exists. This has been the case in the past: one
example is the feudal structure of society in the
Middle Ages, a structure taken over by the Church
so that redemption could be revealed in that social
pattern. Today is no different. If the prototype
(and Church) is representative and unitive for
all mankind in terms of nations, an oekumene,
isn't that same true for institutions? More

specifically, doesn't the Church have an intentional
institutional function, a divinely mandated purpose
among other institutions, and so become a "redemptive
institution"?

In considering the Church as a redemptive
institution we begin to see that the fluid boundaries
between Church and mankind become an operative
principle for ecclesiology. These fluid boundaries
refer not only to membership in the Church, to
individuals; they refer to the structures and
institutions of Church and world as well. At one
level of analysis, the sociological, the Church
assumes worldly structures and institutions, imperial,
feudal, monarchic, democratic, because these are
the available social structures, the "models" in
the sociological sense, that churchmen have to
draw upon. But at another level, this fluidity,
based on the Incarnation, permits the totality of
humanity, not just individuals, but man's whole
world, social and institutional, to participate
in the power, effects and results of the Incarnation.

At a more profound theological level, then,
such fluidity of boundaries means that the Church
assumes the structures of society, becomes concretized
in these structures precisely so that they might
share as well in the redemptive power of Christ.

Fluidity applies not only to an Incarnational
view of the Church but also to an Eschatological
vision. The Church continues the work of Christ,
reaching out to overcome the boundaries between
Church and the world. The blurring of boundaries
between Church and mankind does not deny the
dialectical tension of the Church with the world;
rather it points up the tension involved in the
constant interplay between the power of Redemption
and the structures of mankind that must be brought
to redemption or freedom. The tension consists,
at least in part, in the effort to overcome these
boundaries. Here is the Eschatological vision: the
overcoming of the boundaries that will signify
the ushering in of the Kingdom of God. The

Kingdom is not yet, another aspect of that tension. The world in its very development indicates the direction that the Church must take (this is the wedding of Incarnation and Eschaton) so that the Church can never be satisfied that this particular historical epoch is redeemed or brought into the Kingdom of God, since the Kingdom does not yet exist. Boundaries still remain.

The Church must, however, heed the direction that God indicates by his action in the world.[13] The world causes tension in the Church, a tension between the already that is realized in the Church and the social and historical dimensions of the world that await redemption. And so the world, a locus of God's action along with the Church, by its own dynamic provides a source of tension for the Church.

This tension, of course, stands in direct relationship to the mandate or mission of the Church. Tavard insists on the theological importance of this relationship: "The power to assimilate the needs of the times, to sense the assumptions and desires of mankind at a given period, to hear and to respond to the interrogations addressed to the Church, represents one of the essential qualities of religious truth."[14] It is the direct relationship between the Church and the given historico-social structures that is determinative of the mission and hence of the form of the Church in a given period. For form and function, structure and mission, are always correlative, both sociologically and theologically.

Certainly the Kinghom of God is not the Church, but the purpose of the Church. The Church's mission is the Kingdom: the Church exists for the Kingdom. However, Carl Braaten warns that "there is no relation between the Kingdom of God and the Church that does not include the world."[15] Here we see that blurring of boundaries, the end of frontiers between the Church and the world as the Church sets about its work of preparing for the eschatological kingdom.

We see then that if we do not hold to hard
and fast boundaries between Church and world, we
can understand better the nature and mission of
the Church, both at the Incarnational and
Eschatological poles. It is this underlying
current in much of contemporary ecclesiology
that permits a further deepening and understanding
of both incarnational and eschatological themes.
These themes in turn give us some basic principles
for the development of a theology for a multiform
Church.

INCARNATIONAL PRINCIPLE[16]

Thomas Sheridan has broadly sketched the
"incarnational principle" and its application
to the Church.

> His (God's) choice of the Incarnation
> meant that in order to raise us up to Him,
> He chose first to stoop down to our level.
> He chose to become man, 'in all things made
> like unto his brethren,' (Heb. 2:17), to
> take on a concrete, real human nature
> through all the stages of earthly existence:
> from conception, to birth, to a life filled
> with every human experience except such as
> was incompatible with His divine nature,
> and finally to death, in order to divinize
> this human nature and through it the rest
> of mankind.

> Having once established this incar-
> national principle, God continues to act
> according to it . . . . We see this first
> of all in the Church.[17]

Ben Meyer, in The Church in Three Tenses, con-
firms this point of view about the New Testament.
He maintains that "ecclesial images and titles"[18]
converge on this central point: identification of
the Church with Christ. I would certainly modify
this statement; for not all the New Testament

images and titles focus on this incarnational
aspect. But certainly we find the ultimate attempt
to express this theological principle in the
                of the Pauline literature. The image
invoked may be opaque because the reality behind
the image is too profound, too dense to be encompassed in one kind of imagery. Certainly, however,
there is nothing of such intensity in the Old
Testament or the Inter-Testamental Literature,
so that we see a truly "new" reality struggling
to be expressed. This new reality is the Incarnational Reality.

The application of this principle to the
Church can, of course, lead to excess, especially
to a too facile identification of the Church with
Christ. Paul insists on this distinction between
Christ and the Church: He is the distinct source
of life and its leader or director (see Eph. 1:22-
23). Rather the Incarnational principle is in
itself a call, a requirement and a stimulus to
greater holiness. This has been stressed frequently
in regard to individuals; but the same requirement
based on the Incarnational union must be insisted
upon with respect to the Church. The call to
holiness is institutional and social as well as
individual and personal.

Macquarrie develops the meaning of holiness
in a provocative passage in _Principles_ _of_ _Christian_
Theology: "In more ontological language (than
hortatory) . . . holiness is co-operation with the
letting be of Being, it is the strengthening and
promoting the beings as against the threat of
dissolution. But normally this can be done only
by the maximal participation and involvement in
the life of the world."

Macquarrie, in establishing these basic
Christian principles, does not mean to exclude the
Church itself from following this principle. In
fact, it is the Church that must first and foremost
be holy because of its union with Christ through
the Incarnation. In accordance with the principle

99

of Incarnational holiness, this means that the
Church must not only promote those structures and
institutions that in a given historical context
prevent dissolution; the Church must somehow share
and participate in these institutions in the life
of the world if it is not to avoid its responsibility.

The Incarnation provides mankind with a
fuller understanding of its own purpose and identity:
the Incarnation reveals the full identity of man
in the "letting be of Being". An Incarnational
Church carries on the task of establishing the full
identity of mankind, of man as he is. This
fullness of identity as constituted in Christ is
the content of the Incarnation that must be
extended to man as he is in each historical situation.
Consequently the content of the Incarnation
reaches not just the individual in his or her
relationship to God; it extends to the whole
institutional order.

Following this principle of the Incarnation,
the Church must take on the forms and structures
of the world around her. Just as Jesus assumed
the idiosyncratic particularities of a first
century Palestinian, so the Church must be willing
to take on the institutional particularities of
the historical context in which it finds itself;
for "in her institutional form . . . the Church
is now seen and experienced as the visible form
on earth of Christ's redemptive grace."[20]   That
grace, as universal, must extend to every area of
man's life, including the institutional.

However, the life of the Church is not without
tension; for as we shall see there are several
dimensions of a dialectical tension that the
Church must face in living in the world, not the
least of which is the tension of the Incarnational
principle itself.

The Incarnational principle also demands that
the Church re-evaluate its past history and the
past as it influences current social and institutional

forms that in the contemporary situation should
allow persons to be free, allow beings to be
against the threat of dissolution. This is not
different than saying that the whole history of
the Mosaic covenant had to be re-evaluated in
light of the Incarnation itself. It is the Incarnational principle that lays this imperative on
the Church for every age and for every socio-
cultural milieu.

The Incarnational principle pushes the
Church somewhat further however. The Church cannot
remain an a-historical institution, divorced from
the social and historical changes in the surrounding
milieu; and in following out this principle she
must become involved in history and in society.
This is the real task of the Church; and at the same
time, it raises certain problems of discernment.
How is the Church to become involved in history
without becoming history's accomplice, without
adjustment or compromise of her basic mission?
This leads us to the eschatological dimension of an
ecclesial theology.

ESCHATOLOGICAL ASPECTS OF THE CHURCH

The Church is an historical association,
subject to history as well as influencing history
in a dialectical relationship. Because of its
embeddedness in history, the Church has and will
continue to take on different historical forms.
The Church, as association, is also a sociological
entity and as such, takes on the social forms,
relationships and aspects available from the social
groups of an historical time and place.[21] As a
sociological entity, the Church must be where it
finds itself and cannot retreat from the encounter
with history and history's social institutions.

The Church, then, is involved in history in
its pilgrimage to the eschatological Kingdom of
God. The Church's mandate is related to the
Kingdom, the Church must point to and work for

the Kingdon, but it can do so only by going <u>through</u>
the world.[22] Clearly, this means that in some ways
the Church will also be subject to the forces of the
world. The Church must then both learn how to change,
<u>and</u> at the same time to preserve its identity; and
this learning must take place in a self-conscious
and reflective way. "We are concerned with the
change. . . in which the Church changes itself and
is not merely subjected to change, though of course
both sets of changes mutually affect one another."[23]

This is the focal point of the Incarnation as
well. The Incarnation is God's action embedded and
embodied in history and continuing in history:
this one continuous act of God takes on the form
of history to bring history to its "end". As such,
it is eschatological.[24] Christ unites the Church
to himself by his death and resurrection; it is the
eschatological promise that creates the Church. But
Christ identifies himself with his Church so that
the whole of creation will come to maturity, to
that maturity of which the Incarnation is seed and
beginning. Thus as the Incarnation brought about
ture identity for mankind, so union with and through
the Resurrected Lord brings about full maturity in
Christ, the destiny of men singly and socially.
Only the Resurrection and its eschatological implications provide us with the full grasp of the promise
to mankind in Christ. Thus the Church is meant to
be the sign of the world's destiny: it is precisely
the Incarnational Church in the light of the Lord
of History that is and must be Eschatological.
"It is the 'eschatological community' in the same
way that Christ is the 'eschatological man' -- the
sign of the end or goal."[25]

Following upon this, we see that the human
character of the Church must include "incarnation"
in the institutional life of the world, in those
institutions that seem to have become autonomous
and pluralized. The Church has been called the
Institutional Incarnation"[26] although I would
prefer to speak of it as revealing the institutional
aspect of the Incarnation. As such, the Church

102

must be involved in history; and by this involvement, it points to the end of history. "in this eschatological time, since Christ's exaltation, the Church is at work, bearing fruit through her communion with Christ."[27] The Church is eschatological precisely because it is incarnational.

Because the Church is a socio-historical reality, the forms of the Church can pass away, or be altered in different socio-historical contexts. Yet is is still the fruit of God's continuous and never repented action of the Incarnation and as such is believed to persist through history.[28] This persistence through history, precisely in a variety of altered forms and structures, presages history's fulfillment. "All things will pass away," including the forms and structures of the "institutional incarnation." But God's act remains, bringing history to its end and culmination.

It should be noted that "end" is somewhat equivocal; and can mean "end" in the sense of stop or completion, finis; or it can mean the goal, that toward which a thing is drawn, but which itself is still a dynamic reality, influencing that which it draws or attracts. It is this second sense of entelechy that the eschatological end of history refers to.[29] Thus Moltmann can speak of this end or goal as "the beginning of the eschatological transformation of the world by its creator."[30] The Church is involved in this transformation, for the Church is the sign and instrument of the Kingdom.

The eschatological responsibility of the Church to world and society means that the Church must meet the world and its institutions in history, must in fact go through these institutions of time, history and culture, for the Church cannot get to the Kingdom without going through the world. This view is partially in agreement with the radical theologians of secularity, who, as Shiner states, "see the task of faith then is not to transform secularity."[31] Faith rather is to "keep

103

man's responsibility limited to immanent and partial ends."[32]   I believe that this is acceptable
if understood to mean that human institutions are
immanent -- i.e., they do not ultimately transcend
the human anthropological condition -- and partial --
i.e., no institution is final in human history.

However a "secular theology" can be interpreted
exclusively as an incarnational theology. This
would be a limited theology and restrict the mission
of the Church to work not only in in the world but
only for the world. The Church is concerned with
human institutions; but this concern, as eschatological, looks beyond human institutions to God's
Kingdom which is God's creation not man's, as are
human institutions. The Church must be provisional
and see the world as provisional, and thus remain
open to the transcendent.[33]

Because the Kingdom is the result of God's
power, we cannot be certain of its ultimate contours.
But in relationship to human institutions, we
can be sure of one proximate feature that is
simultaneously eschatological: theological or
absolute freedom. The proximate content of the
Kingdom of which the Church is witness and instrument is such freedom as a hallmark of the Kingdom.
In the final section of this chapter, I shall discuss
more fully the place of freedom in this ecclesiology.
Here it is important to note that the Church's
eschatological involvement with human institutions
is to bring them to respond to and to become
proximate loci of freedom.

I wish to admit here an eschatological interpretation that sees the relationship of all creation,
including human creation, to the Kingdom. The theology of secularity accepts the world, but in this
perspective the world is accepted not only for
itself but to be brought to eschatological fulfillment; and this fulfilled world will be the
Kingdom when God wills it. The Church enters
into society to prepare for the Kingdom, as the
agent of the Kingdom; not to baptize social

institutions but to show them the way to fulfillment
and to insist upon freedom. This is the histroical
responsibility of the Church.

Shiner continues in his analysis of secularity,
"What the Church in particular has to offer the
world is not ethical principles or advice but the
Word of God calling free men into being. Through
such 'mature' men and women the Church will be
able to remind the world of its own worldliness
and secularity."[34] The Church enters into
history and its institutions to bring people to
this kind of maturity in history. But the Church
also must remind human institutions that they are
called to this maturity, "fullness in Christ."
We have now a clearer understanding of the fact
that we are not "saved" or "freed" one by one,
but in consort or congress with each other. We
are saved through our human institutions not apart
from them. The Church then must initiate the
transformation of those institutions; it is this
kind of salvation, of salvic activity that until
now the Church has been reluctant to engage in.[35]
But it is this transformation of institutions
that will usher in the eschaton, the
completion or fullness of God's action in history.
This is then the eschatological responsiblity
of the Church. But eschatological accountability
means that the Church is always a Church under
judgment, -- the judgment of the Kingdom. On
the other hand, the Church too exercises judgment,
judgment on the world and its social institutions
-- including her own involvement in those institutions. The Church is both judge and to be
judged. The Church is "gifted" for the sake of
the Kingdom. As well as institutional incarnation,
the Church is also the continuous incarnation of
charismata.

CHARISMATIC STRUCTURE OF CHRISTIANITY

As the Church moves toward this eschatological
fulfillment, she is provided with certain aids,

"graces", on the pilgrimage that leads to the Kingdom. Chief among these, we are now beginning to realize, are the gifts, the charismata, the pneumatika that have been poured out upon the Church in the outpouring of the Spirit. This new recognition about the "charismatic structure of the Church"[36] stems in part from the renewal in Biblical theology and in part from the renewal in ecclesiology.

The particular focus here, however, is to consider a well-rounded theology of the charismata as they might apply not to individual Christians nor to the universal Church[37] but to various groupings of Christians within the Church and to the way Christians might see themselves as group-gifted in the society of which they are members.

These gifts of the Spirit, charismata, are given in the outpouring of the Spirit upon the Church for the needs of the Church. In fact, in the Pauline view of these gifts, they are basic to the structure and function of the Church. To speak of the "charismatic structure" of the Church does not exclude other ways of viewing the Church; but to neglect this aspect of the Church is to allow a lacuna in a total view of the Church in its constitutive structure.[38]

In the Pauline view, then, what are the main functions and what is the basic understanding of these pneumatic gifts in an ecclesial perspective? (The gifts of the Spirit, in fact, have no place outside this ecclesial perspective.) In the first place, it seems obvious that the gifts are given for the needs of the community. It is in the service of the community that recipients of the gifts are to exercise first of all this outpouring of power. The dogmatic Constitution on the Church of Vatican II makes this point clear:

> By these gifts he (the Holy Spirit)
> makes them (the faithful of every rank)
> fit and ready to undertake the various
> tasks and duties which contribute

> toward the renewal and building up of
> the Church . . . . These charisms
> whether they be the more outstanding or
> the more simple and widely diffused,
> are to be received with thanksgiving
> and consolation for they are especially
> suited to and useful for the needs of
> the Church.[39]

But the needs of the Church are served not
only by individuals in the Church, but by various
groupings in the Church as well. These groups
surely serve for the "renewal and building up
of the Church"; there seems no reason to exclude
them from receiving other charisms as well for the
life of the Church.[40]

In Pauline theology as well, we know that
every Christian is anointed by the Spirit and has
received his or her share of gifts. This seems
to be the view as well of John and of Luke,
especially in his account in Acts.

> According to Acts 2, the Spirit has
> been poured out "upon all flesh". Who-
> ever has received the Spirit, shares in
> the gifts of the Spirit. The charisma is
> therefore not the privilege of a few elect,
> based on religious "enthusiasm" or on
> office, but of the whole Church as the
> community of all the faithful.[41]

Once we acknowledge both the universality of
the charismata and the possibility of a variety of
communal structures and groupings within the
Church (without as yet specifying the exact nature
of the groupings), it seems fair to maintain that
these groups or structured communities would
receive special gifts from the Spirit in accord
with their own work in the community of believers.

The Church, however, exists for more than
simply its own sake. The Church exists primarily
for the Kingdom of God and is commissioned to

107

carry out the work of its mandate in the world of building for the Kingdom. "This means that the community is in no way self-oriented."[42] Not only the Church as a whole, not only individual Christians, but other sub-groups and organizations within the Church exist to carry out this work of service and mission. "And God is able to make all grace abound in you, so that always having ample means, you may abound in every good work." (2 Cor. 9:8)

Paul seems to be addressing this very issue: every kind of work is to be done in the Christian community for the sake of the Kingdom, and Christians have been given ample means for this. These more than sufficient aids must be given as well to those groups in the Church that are intent on carrying on the work of the Church in the world.

This leads to the next point in a theology of charisms: diversity. The Church is involved in a variety of actions in the world, and when the various lists of charismata drawn up by Paul are consulted (especially 1 Cor. 12:28-31; Rom. 12:6-8; Eph. 4:11-16) one becomes aware of the great variety of these gifts in the Pauline theology of charisms. In fact, "this infinite variety of the charismata implies their unlimited distribution in the Church."[43]

Since this work of the Church is carried on not only by individuals and not even by the Church as a whole, but principally in our day by various groups in the Church, it is safe to conclude that these groups too share in this "unlimited distribution" of gifts for building up, for service, for witness and mission. "The presence of great variety which must exist in the Church . . . is brought about by the rights and exercises of supernatural gifts within the charismatic structure of the Christian community."[44]

However, it is not enough to apply a theology of charisms to groups and communities that have arisen in the Church. A charismatic ecclesiology forces us to recognize that these groups will arise in the Church by the very nature of the "charismatic structure of the Church".

> To St. Paul the Church of the living Christ does not appear as some kind of administrative organization, but as a living web of gifts, of charisms, or ministries. The Spirit is given to every individual Christian, the Spirit who gives his gifts, his charisms to each and every one "different as they are allotted to us by God's grace."(Rom. 12:6)[45]

And to every different Christian group, we must add.

The nature of the Church, then, is charismatic and once we see that the manner in which Christians act in the world is communal, we see that it is the charisms, the gifts of the Holy Spirit, that have led to the formation of these structures and groups. It is <u>because</u> the Church is charismatic by nature that charismatic groups come into existence to carry out the work for which the Church was established. This is a way that both believers and those who do not yet believe can come to recognize the Church in all her manifestations.

In the Pauline view of the Church, it is not simply the individual who is the recipient of the charisms, nor is it some "abstract" Church. Paul, of course, sees the local congregations as the locus and receptacle for these gifts, but he goes further.

> For Paul every congregation is a charismatic community, a body shaped and informed by the Spirit of Christ and His gifts. First Corinthians 12 is not a description of the Church as it once was in one place. It is a statement of our Lord's abiding will and expectation for

the Church in all times in every place
. . . . The Church, the congregation
of believers, in any place, if it is
alive at all, lives by the charismatic
infusion of the Spirit.[46]

The point to be made here then is that the
Church, in Paul's view, must be charismatic: that
is foundational. And the "charismatic structure"
of the Church means that localized groups of
Christians qua groups are recipients of these
gifts for their own needs and for their mission
in the world. The relationship of groups of
Christians to their mission in the world is, of
course, what interests us in a theology for a
multiform Church.

COUNTER-INSTITUTIONAL ECCLESIOLOGY

Many theologians of "church structures," not
to mention administrators and "canon lawyers,"
object to a theology of charisms in any form
because it seems to justify an anarchic situation
in the Church. Of course, this theology can be
absurd; but as Karl Rahner establishes at
length in his provocative monograph, The Dynamic
Element in the Church, it is one Lord Who gives
both office and charism in the Church, Who establishes
both "institutional" and "charismatic" structures
in the Church, and "harmony between the two
'structures' of the Church, the institutional and
the charismatic, can only be guaranteed by the
one Lord of both, and by him alone, that is to
say, charismatically."[47]

Rahner extends this line of thought in a later
remarkable essay, "Institution and Freedom," in
which he lays the foundations for a theology of
counter-institutions, ecclesial and "secular".[48]
It is this theology of counter-ecclesial institutions
that certainly provides a basis for a pluriform
ecclesiology and which is also closely related to
the theology of charisms, for just such counter-

institutions depend on the gifts and guidance of the Spirit which certainly will not be lacking for the building up of the Church.

Theology, Rahner maintains, is concerned with institutions because institutions are instruments of freedom and of constraint. Freedom and constraint are theological issues, although Rahner is careful to distinguish theological freedom from social freedom. Nevertheless, "This theological freedom must be seen . . . in its inner relationship to social freedom."[49]

Social freedom, being the condition and aspiration for a more human and better world for man, "is a concrete expression of that desire and aspiration to see God's Kingdom appear in its final power, and this desire is another word for faith."[50] But, Rahner points out, it is the very paradox of institutions that they both provide the possibility of freedom and the necessity of constraint in society. Men create institutions to overcome chaotic anarchy and thus provide an area of free activity; but to provide this freedom, paradoxically constraint becomes necessary and thus the freedom provided by human institutions is never absolute.

In this ambiguity of institutions which both provide an arena for freedom and at the same time place limits on free activity the desire or hope for absolute freedom arises, a freedom that would allow man to move beyond this ambiguity of the human limiting situation. This absolute freedom is what has been promised in the Incarnation and which is awaited by Christians in the expectation of the eschatological Kingdom. In other words, God is the source of this perfected freedom; but God is "also the origin of all structure"[51] which in the present situation makes freedom possible. Thus Rahner argues that theology must consider institutions at that level and from that perspective that is concerned with the desire of man for freedom and in light of the centrality of the idea of freedom in the New Testament; for freedom "is what has been gained by a history of salvation involving every man and all mankind, something realized already as event and stretching out now toward its coming fulfillment."[52]

Because "a man should realize and live out this inner liberation of his freedom beyond the ambivalent institutional forms this freedom creates," he may in fact and in creative faith transform or bring into existence institutions that are more "transparent to freedom,"[53] institutions whose structure better serves freedom, which is in fact an act of faith and hope in God who is author of both freedom and structure.

These reformed or new institutions can in fact exist for the "sole purpose of preserving freedom against other institutions."[54] Rahner cites as principal examples certain legal institutions such as ex officio counsels for the Defense and Courts of Appeal. It is imporant to extend this notion to the Church.

The absolute hope for freedom and its promise in the New Testament are in fact eschatological dimensions of the Christian life. As such, they are related to the Kingdom, for the fulfillment of the Kingdom of God is in fact the locus for absolute freedom. But the way to the Kingdom is through the Church, as we have seen. The "institution . . . expressly organized here as a means of counter-institutional struggle for freedom"[55] is an ecclesial or proto-ecclesial institution. But it is certainly, although not exclusively, the work of the Church to serve freedom by affirming this faith and hope in constructing counter-institutions that in furthering social freedom inevitably provide the possibility for "theological" freedom in the Kingdom of God.

Extending the theology of Rahner dealing with counter-institutional ecclesiology as well as the

theology of charismatic dynamis, we can see the
critical function that is clearly a crucial aspect
of counter-institutional ecclesiology. The
Church as counter-institution not only passes
judgment on those institutions that hinder freedom;
the Church as gifted and counter-institutional
poses a crisis also for the institutional forms
of the Church itself. The Church must face
the question: do these institutional ecclesial
forms promote man's freedom and reveal his
destiny?

The counter-institutional Church provides the
critical thrust, the crisis that precipitates
judgment; and the work of judgment is also a work
of the Spirit, a charisma, for judgment and
discernment are fruits of the Spirit. Thus when
an institutional form of the Church fails to reveal
the Church's own destiny, i.e., when it is not
eschatological, then it is brought under judgment
by a counter-institutional thrust, a development
in the Church itself that is the work of the
Spirit.

Thus far, this theology of counter-institutions has relied on and extended the theology
of institution and freedom as developed by Karl
Rahner. However, other theologians have addressed
this problem, although not all have approached
it with the same profundity or breadth as Rahner.
Two confirmatory (and earlier) statements, per-
taining specifically to politics but applicable
across a range of social institutions, were
expressed in the World Council of Churches volume
edited by Z. K. Matthews, Responsible Government
in a Revolutionary Age.56 Here again we see the
relationship of counter-institutions to freedom,
judgment and destiny.

Max Kohnstamm, following Reinhold Niebuhr,
states:

> The political philosophy of the West
> urges that, for every power, there should
> be a counter-balancing power, and that
> there should be freedom to place every
> center of power and ideology under review . . .
> Whatever material and spiritual influences

have shaped it, whatever part the Bible
may have played among these influences,
the important point is that the view of
man on which the West's institutions and
political philosophy is based allows both
for the goodness of man's creation and
for his involvement in the ambiguities of
life.57

This is a brief statement of the principle
for which Rahner is attempting to provide theological justification. First we should note that
Kohnstamm sees this as an institutional tradition
in the West, although his specific application is
to politics. Secondly, as we have seen, institutions
by the very fact of their power of constraint
limit the freedom of individuals. Such limitation
raises theological issues which involve ecclesial
or proto-ecclesial "counter-institutionalization".
This kind of scrutiny brought to bear on the
constraining power of institutions can be regarded
as ecclesial or churchly activity, i.e., the work
of the Church in discerning and overcoming the
forces that impede the absolute freedom of the
Kingdom of God.

Another theologican from Eastern Europe, J. B.
Soucek, points out:

What is needed everywhere is the renewal
of the churches, which means the genuine
Christianization of us all.

But this cannot be achieved by
simply taking note of this truth and
waiting for renewal. Renewal can come
only within the framework of a determined,
devoted effort to work for the aims that
we have recognized as imperative for our
Christian conscience. In this respect,
the Christian Peace Conference, with its
aim of reconciliation, may be an instrument of the coming renewal of the Church.58

This is, once again, a statement for the necessity of counter-institutions -- without that name as such -- using an example drawn from within the Church itself. Perhaps the necessity for counter-institutions became obvious earlier to theologians who lived through the Stalinist era: the Church may have been the chief source of counter-institutions in a constraining social system. At any rate, an ecclesial counter-institution need not originate directly from the institutionalized Church nor need it be completely distinct from the social group to which it addresses itself as a counter-institution. Recall in this regard Rahner's examples of legal counter-institutions.

Perhaps we can see a forerunner of this theology of counter-institutions in the Free Church theology, especially as interpreted by modern theologians of the Free Church tradition. While it is true that the Anabaptist movement was in general a tendency toward separation from the world, the theology behind the movement certainly supports a "counter-institution" theology. "Anabaptism roots ultimately on perpetual spiritual re-creation which derives its authority from the work of the Spirit among men thereby united, and not from ecclesiastical structure."[59] Franklin Littell thinks that the emergence of this "Third Type" of Protestantism sets the context for explaining "the development of the type of Church-life characteristic of America."[60] Certainly the voluntary association has been the model of the Church in America and the Free Church is the ecclesial forerunner of this model.

CONCLUSION

An integrated ecclesiology shows the relationship between various ways of understanding the Church today and that these various ways of ecclesial self-understanding, far from being opposed to a polystructured Church, are in fact supportive of such a view. The relationship between

incarnational and eschatological and between these
and charismatic and counter-institutional theological themes show that these different strands
in contemporary ecclesiology reinforce each other;
moreover they provide the basis for the ecclesiology
of a multiform Church. Nevertheless, that such a
view has not been present in a well-articulated
way in previous ecclesiological understanding is
not a judgment on the past; rather, as we have
indicated previously, the past did not require
this kind of self-conscious ecclesiology (although
it needed an appropriate self-conscious ecclesiology).
It is only with the possibility of a pluralistic
society that it has become necessary to think
of the presence and implications of a multiform
Church.

It would seem that today special emphasis
should be given to these ecclesial themes:
incarnational, eschatological, charismatic and
counter-institutional. These are clearly central
issues among contemporary theologians; further,
they preclude a reduction of the Church to one
or a few Scriptural images or doctrinal constructs
and thus provide for an open vision of the Church
without compromising any essential ecclesial
characteristics. Thus, any structure or form
of the Church need not take on an air of finality;
at the same time there is no room for a belittling
disparagement of the provisional characteristics
of the Church such as pilgrim or sign, (as some
criticize in Brunner or other dialectical theologians).

Further, these particular ecclesial themes
are important given the world of socio-cultural
pluralism. By this I mean that if we accept the
secular autonomy, even the attempts at imperialism
of modern social institutions, the Church can no
longer emphasize her institutional or structural
aspects if she is to be credible in the modern
world. Surely the Church will continue to have
institutional aspects; but if socio-cultural

116

pluralism defines the social contours of our world, then the Church can best present herself not as one among other competing institutions but with those characteristics that both bring social institutions to fuller development and judge social institutions for not promoting that development. Moreover these emphases provide a check agains neo-triumphalism, for the Church is also subject to judgment and not above eschatological criticism.

1. There are a few concluding remarks that should be made at the end of this chapter. First, diversity is not new in the Church; but we must now think of ways not only to preserve diversity in the face of new patterns of institutionalization; we must make a real attempt to <u>understand</u> the nature of diversity as gift or grace. This is what Paul means when he speaks of the Body having many members; but we tend to interpret this only in an individualistic way. We must now also see this in an institutional way and be careful not to allow an institutional uniformity to develop contrary to Christian teaching. "The genuine diversity-in-unity of the body of Christ needs to be defended against uniformity just as much as against divisiveness."[61] The pressures for uniformity come from institutionalization and so the preservation of diversity-in-unity must also require an institutional pattern built-in, a pattern that has its theology drawn up in accord with the principles of this chapter.

2. Secondly, this theology of the Church builds on the classical sociological tradition of Weber and Troeltsch, but I believe goes beyond their view theologically. Fuse summarizes the classical view:

> Troeltsch summarizes the problems and dilemmas of the institutionalized religion (the Church) as follows: the central ideals and values of Christianity "cannot be realized within this world apart from compromise" and therefore the history of Christianity "becomes the story

117

of a constantly renewed search for this compromise, and a fresh opposition to this spirit of compromise." What Troeltsch is suggesting here is that the history of the Christian Church is best understood in terms of two contradictory yet complimentary tendencies in a dialectical process: compromise with the world and tension with the world.[62]

The theology presented here, rather than proposing a new form of compromise, in fact attempts to bring out the tension of the Church in the world. The Church, while having its being in the forms of the world, never completely loses itself or its identity by compromise. Instead by adaptation the Church seeks to become recognizable as Church and relevant for the social situation. The Church continues to preserve its identity as belonging in the world by its tension with the world.[63] The Church that succumbs to compromise is no longer, or at least for a while not yet truly Church.

Tension continues to exist in another way, because as the Church takes different forms, these forms are in critical but positive relationship with each other.

3. This leads to a third issue that can be raised here. This polymorphic theology of the Church has certain ecumenical ramifications. Just as these various forms can make the Church more consciously self-critical, so in the past various Christian groups and denominations have provided a basis for the self-examination of other Christian groups. We have already seen how the ecclesial tradition of the Free Churches provides a certain basis for this view of the diversity in the Church. Orthodox theology as well looks to a varied structure. Evdokimov notes: "Not the conciliar structure but the catholicity and collegiality of all are the notes of the Church; the historical expression may vary."[64]

118

We may also say: The socio-cultural expressions
may vary. If we think of catholicity as tending
to all aspects of man's life and collegiality
meaning the contribution of each, we can see how an
Orthodox view of the Church is in harmony with
this theology. Here we can say that we have the
theological basis for self-conscious positive
criticism of "Church" as institution. Further
ecumenical considerations will be discussed in the
final chapter.

4. One final issue should be mentioned here in
light of the preceding chapter. The social
psychological implications of modern institutions
have been explored in depth by social scientists,
and sometimes deplored for the alienation these
institutions have engendered. In light of this
theological exploration the Church must do more
than merely devise new structures; it must "be
prepared to stand aside and encourage . . . fellow-
Christians to work out for themselves what the
Gospel means for them today."[65]   But in working
out the meaning of the Gospel, what shape might
the Church take? We will see a variety of new
and renewed structures, not hand-me-downs from
a previous age or from a bureaucratic superstructure.
This the the subject of the next chapter.

REFERENCES

1. Tavard, George. The Changing Church. Glen Rock: Paulist Press, 1966. p. 15.

2. Berger, Peter and Luckmann, Thomas P. Secularization and Pluralism", p. 73.

3. Ibid.

4. Ibid.

5. Yinger, J. Milton, "Pluralism, Religion and Secularism," Journal for the Scientific Study of Religion 6:1. 1967: 17-18.

6. Luckmann, Thomas. The Invisible Religion. p. 85.

7. Williams, Jr., Robin M. American Society, 3d ed. New York: Alfred Knopf, 1970. p. 301. (emphasis added.)

8. It should be noted here, in connection with discussion of the sociocultural system, that Bellah in "Religious Evolution" indicates that the historic or "great" religions gave rise to a four-class social system: a political-military elite, a cultural-religious elite, a rural lower-status group (peasantry), and an urban lower-status group (merchants and artisans). This was not pluralism in the sense I mean here; but more likely (Bellah believes certainly) developed into a division of power between political and religious realms, a kind of caste situation.

9. While Berger and Luckmann differ in their definitions of religion, their fundamental analysis prior to arriving at any definition is very similar, as would be expected.

10. Barrett, William W. "Subsidiarity, Order
    and Freedom in the Church," in Coriden, James
    A., ed. The Once and Future Church. New
    York: Alba House, 1971. p. 212.

11. Schillebeeckx, Edward. "The Church and Mankind"
    in Schillebeeckx, E., ed. The Church and
    Mankind, Concilium. Vol. I. Glen Rock: Paulist
    Press, 1965. p. 81.

12. Cf., e.g., ibid. p. 98.

13. See Cox, Harvey. The Secular City. New York:
    MacMillan, 1965, in this regard.

14. Tavard, George. The Changing Church. p. 15.

15. Braaten, Carl. "The Church in Ecumenical and
    Cultural Crossfire," Theology Digest 15:4
    Winter, 1967: 286.

16. Obviously the "Incarnational"aspect of the
    Church is a study in itself. In Catholic
    theology, see, e.g., Mersch, Emile. The
    Theology of the Mystical Body, trans. by
    Cyril Vollert, St. Louis: Herder, 1951:   and
    in Protestant theology, Knox, John. The
    Church and the Reality of Christ. New York:
    Harper and Row, 1962, esp. Chapter 4, "The
    Church and the Incarnation".

17. Sheridan, Thomas L. The Church in the New
    Testament. Glen Rock: Paulist Press, 1962.
    pp. 22-23.

18. Meyer, Ben. The Church in Three Tenses.
    New York: Doubleday, 1971. p. 21. See
    Schlink, Edmund. The Coming Christ and the
    Coming Church. Philadelphia: Fortress Press,
    1968. pp. 96-98, for a view of the Church
    that has Trinitarian aspects and not simply
    a Christological relationship.

19. Macquarrie, John. Principles of Christian
    Theology. New York: Charles Scribners'
    Sons, 1966. pp. 363-364.

20. Schillebeckx, E. Revelation and Theology.
    Vol. II, trans. by N. D. Smith. New York:
    Sheed and Ward, 1968. p. 133.

21. See the perceptive work by Stinchcombe on
    the relationship of the time of the origin
    of an institution and its subsequent
    development. Stinchcombe, Arthur L.
    "Bureaucratic and Craft Administration of
    Production," Administrative Science
    Quarterly, 4:2. September, 1959: 168-187.
    The argument is elaborated in detail in
    Stinchcombe, "Social Structure and Organizations,"
    in March, James, ed. Handbook of Organizations.
    Chicago: Rand McNally & Co., 1965. pp. 142-193.

    Serendipitously Stanley Udy proposed similar
    conclusions in The Organization of Work.
    New Haven, Conn.: Human Relations Area Files,
    1959. However, Udy's work is neither as
    insightful nor as free of error as Stinch-
    combe's.

22. Cf. Braaten, Carl, "The Church in Ecumenical
    and Cultural Crossfire."

23. Rahner, Karl. The Christian of the Future.
    New York: Herder and Herder, 1967. p. 11.

24. Cf. Knox, John. The Church and the Reality of
    Christ. pp. 85-86.

25. Williams, Colin W. The Church, New
    Directions in Theology Today, Vol. IV.
    Philadelphia: The Westminster Press, 1968.
    pp. 73-74.

26. The term is Schillebeeckx, Revelation and
    Theology, Vol. II. p. 135.

27. Schnackenburg, The Church in the New Testament. p. 123.

28. Thus Heaven and earth will pass away; my words will not pass away." (Luke 21:33) "On this rock I will build my Church and the gates of hell shall not prevail against it." (Matt. 16:18-19)

29. Cf. Meyer, Ben. The Church in Three Tenses. pp. 50-51.

30. Moltmann, Jurgen. The Crucified God: The Cross of Christ as the Foundation and Criticism of Christian Theology. New York: Harper & Row, 1974. p. 162.

31. Shiner, Larry, "Toward a Theology of Secular-ization," Journal of Religion 45 (1965): 288.

32. Ibid.

33. See Haughey, John C. "Church and Kingdom: Ecclesiology in the Light of Eschatology," Theological Studies 29:1. March, 1968: 72-86.

34. Ibid. p. 289.

35. This theology has parallels in the Latin American "theology of liberation". Lucio Gera sees the mission of the Church as trans-lating values into "the outward forms of organization, institutions, structure". The quotation is from a summary by Jose Miguez Bonino on page 66 of Doing Theology in a Revolutionary Situation. Philadelphia: Fortress Press, 1975. See also Chapter 4, "The Theology of Liberation," and Chapter 7, "Kingdom of God, Utopia, and Historical Engagement" in Bonino.

36. The title of a provactive article by Hans
    Kung in The Church and Ecumenism, Concilium,
    Vol. 4, Hans Kung, ed. New York: Paulist
    Press, 1965. pp. 41-61.

37. See De Ecclesia: The Constitution on the
    Church, Vatican Council II, paragraph 12
    for a clear, concise ecclesial statement
    on this aspect of "charismatic theology".

38. See Kung, Hans, "The Charismatic Structure
    of the Church," esp. p. 54.

39. De Ecclesia: The Constitution on the Church,
    paragraph 12.

40. Examples come readily to mind from various
    theological traditions, e.g., the rise of
    the mendicant orders in the 13th century or
    of the conventicles in the 16th.

41. Kung, Hans, "Charismatic Structure" Kung
    continues (p. 58): "Where a church or a
    community thrives only on office holders and
    not on all the members, one may well wonder
    in all seriousness whether the Spirit has
    not been thrown out with the charismata."

42. Koupal, William, "Charism: A Relational
    Concept", Worship 42:9 (Nov., 1968): 542.

43. Kung, Hans, "Charismatic Structure", p. 54.

44. Barrett, William W., "Subsidiarity, Order
    and Freedom in the Church," pp. 246-247.
    (Emphasis added.)

45. Suenens, Cardinal Leon, "The Charismatic
    Dimensions of the Church," in Kung, Hans,
    Congar, Yves, O.P., O'Hanlon, Daniel, S.J.,
    eds. Council Speeches of Vatican II. Glen
    Rock: Paulist Press, 1964. p. 31.

46. Bartling, Walter J. "The Congregation of Christ -- A Charismatic Body: An Exegetical Study of 1 Corinthians 12", Concordia Theological Monthly 40:2 (Feb., 1969): 69.

47. Rahner, Karl. The Dynamic Element in the Church. Montreal: Palm Publishers, 1964. p. 52. Rahner states later on in this essay (p. 70): "The official hierarchy must not be surprised or annoyed if there is stirring in the life of the Spirit before this has been scheduled in the Church's ministries . . . . Canon law concerning equity and the force of custom contra or praeter legem might be thought out from the point of view of this charismatic element in the Church."

48. Rahner, Karl, "Institution and Freedom: Some Theological and Sociological Reflections," Social Studies: Irish Journal of Sociology, 1:2 (March, 1972): 124-136. This essay was first delivered as a paper at University College, Dublin in March, 1971. The text of the delivered address contains some important methodological prologoumena not included in the printed version. In quoting the essay, I will quote the printed version and indicate a quotation from the manuscript only if it is not in the printed version in this way: Manuscript only, p. n.

49. Rahner, Karl, "Institution and Freedom," Manuscript only, p. 2. Rahner develops this relationship which I am summarizing in the Manuscript only. pp. 1-3. The introduction of the printed article, p. 124, is taken from the first page of the manuscript.

50. Ibid. p. 124.

51. Ibid. Manuscript only, p. 3.

52. Ibid. p. 125.

53. Ibid. p. 134.

54. Ibid. p. 135.

55. Ibid.

56. Matthews, Zebediah Keodirelang, ed.
    Responsible Government in a Revolutionary
    Age. New York: Association Press, 1966.

57. Kohnstamm, Max, "The West and the Search
    for Peace in the Nuclear Age", in Matthews,
    Z. K., ed. Responsible Government in a
    Revolutionary Age. p. 75.

58. Soucek, J. B., "Eastern Europe and the
    West in the Search for Peace", in Matthews,
    Z. K. ed., ibid. p. 111.

59. Peackey, Paul, "Anabaptism and Church
    Organization", Mennonite Quarterly Review
    33:3 (1956): 217. (Emphasis added.)

60. Littell, Franklin Hamlin. The Anabaptist
    View of the Church, 2d ed., rev. and enl.
    Boston: Starr King Press, 1958. p. 79.

61. Macquarrie, John. Principles of Christian
    Theology. p. 361.

62. Fuse, Toyomasa, "Religious Institutionalization",
    in Metz, J. B., ed. Faith and the World of
    Politics, Concilium, Vol 36. New York:
    Paulist Press, 1968. pp. 150-151.

63. I believe that Troeltsch labored in part
    under a mistaken theology of the Church
    but that is not the argument in this mono-
    graph.

126

64. Evdokimov, Paul, "Fundamental Desires of the Orthodox Church vis-a-vis the Catholic Church", in Kung, Hans, ed. Do We Know the Others? Concilium, Vol. 14. New York: Paulist Press, 1966. p. 72.

65. "Alienation in Church and Society", Herder Correspondence 5:7 (July, 1968): 196.

CHAPTER 5

THE REAL CHURCH IN THE REAL WORLD

An integral view of ecclesiology provides not only an adequate justification and foundation for a multiform Church; it may in fact demand such a Church. If God is indeed out in front, leading his people, as Cox argues in The Secular City,[1] then the American social experience of pluralism may be bringing us back to a theological understanding that had been underdeveloped in the history of Christendom. What Mirgeler calls the "sociological misunderstanding of the Church"[2] may have prevented the Church from pursuing a more total truth. This "sociological misunderstanding" refers to the Church's attachment to certain historical forms which render it less permeable to the transcendence it is supposed to mediate. For the Church must prepare men for the unexpected, that which is not within the normal range of experience. The transcendent involves "making all things new"[3] and if the Church is not open to that which is beyond familiar dimensions of reality, it might lose its credibility for some or many. Such openness implies that anyone "who believes in God cannot regard any structure as unchangeable and unconditional, so that faith in God should entail a great openness to the future."[4]

This leads us to the concluding issue in the previous chapter. Christians have to work out for themselves the meaning of the Gospel in their own lives. While they are not required to do this without significant aid, Christians will develop structures from their own experience which are not necessarily all alike. It is their own experience in the world that will provide the ground and basis for transcendence and for evangelical service in the normal Christian

129

existence. Christians, in this view, will think
about developing their own human ways of meeting
the world. They will see this as God's way, for
it is accepting responsibility for their own lives
and destiny. It is accepting responsibility for
the Kingdom.

This is somewhat at variance with both a
traditional, sociological and theological view.
Theologically the rationale was not only that
the Church in its essence, form and structure
was a given, either by God or man, but "the
understanding of society in classical and pre-
modern times always implies a religious goal of
society."[5] This older understanding of religion
and by implication of its institutional form has
given way to a new theological understanding
which poses a certain dilemma for the Church:
the "churches" are seeking influence in a world
"with many powers and many values besides their
own"[6] which other values they nevertheless
affirm. What is the application of theology, of
a theological ecclesiology to this condition,
new in our time?

This condition also represents a sociological
shift. We have seen that the development of
modern institutions constitutes a qualitatively
different form of society,[7] so that it is
impossible any longer to view religious institutions
in some a-historical sense, as divorced from the
impact that occurs on other institutions in a
society such as ours. Braaten insists on this
historical embeddedness: "The structures of the
Church in primitive Christianity were culturally
appropriate; they were not experienced either by
those already Christian or by the new converts
to be culturally anachronistic. Structures in
the Church run parallel to structures in society."[8]

It is this same kind of parallelism that the
Church must consciously construct today. It is
not possible either theologically or sociologically
to absolutize one or even several institutional

patterns. In the pluralistic situation there are many legitimating factors that in fact lead to a variety of world views and hence diverse social forms, even antagonistic ones. But in a pluralistic society there is still an appeal to a guiding norm that checks each institution and provides the measure for judging the institution.[9]

The question here is: how is it possible to justify the presence of the Church in and within a variety of institutions which are not only diverse but at times even antagonistic among themselves? First of all we must look briefly at the relationship between sociology and theology and then we can proceed to the theological issues involved.

THEOLOGY and SOCIOLOGY

We have presented the case that "the complex society of the modern world is characterized by numerous large-scale organizations, vast economic and political associations . . . marked by division of function and specialization."[10] Now because "the religious life is so interwoven with social circumstances that the formulation of theology is necessarily conditioned by these (circumstances),"[11] we would expect to find, first, religious life itself developing from the social conditions of modern society, and second, a theology that not only reflected but was applicable to this modern social situation. What we seem to have is a new sociological soil in which the truths of the gospel are to be realized; but what seems to be crucial in this situation is the development of a new style of institution, or a new way of entering institutions that will "effect an almost complete restructuring of religion in its traditional form."[12] It is this restructuring that occupies our attention and refers to the institutional patterning of religion in contemporary society.

We know that ekklesia, the eschatological community of salvation, takes and has taken many

131

forms. Kung points out a Pauline justification
for this and remarks "even small house communities
are referred to by Paul as ekklesia (Rom. 16:5;
Philem. 25; cf. Col. 4:15), and may be listed
alongside larger communities (1 Cor. 16:19)."[13]
But it is not merely that the Church can assume
several forms that are givens from the surrounding
society; the Church can create new forms in
response to the situation in which it exists.
Kung emphasizes the human aspect of the Church:
"Ekklesia grows from below, can be organized,
is the product of development and progress and
dialectic, in short is definitely the work of man."[14]

1. Two points need to be noted in reference to
Kung's last statement. First the Church, as man's
work, is the result of a dialectical engagement
with the world. The restructuring of the religious
institution demands a certain tension, for the
Church must continue to retain her identity as
she is presented in the evangelical witness.
The critical issue is always: "How far religious
insights may be received and incorporated into
the developing ideologies"[15] of the various
institutions of modern society? H. Richard
Niebuhr pursues the fundamental difficulty:
"Each religious group gives expression to that
code which forms the morale of the political or
economic class it represents. They function as
political and class institutions, not as Christian
churches."[16] Pluralism means the existence of
a variety of value systems, which inhere in somewhat different institutions than the class institutions of stratification that Niebuhr describes.
Nevertheless, what the Church must do is translate
the Christian message for each group rather than
become the "group's Church". Lonergan addresses
the issue in the context of evangelism: "To
preach the gospel to all men calls for at least
as many men as there are different places and
times, and it requires each of them to get to
know the people to whom he is sent, their manners
and styles and ways of thought and speech. There
follows a manifold pluralism."[17] To extend

Lonergan's principle, the modern "places and times" are modern institutional structures that pervade our lives; and the individual can never be as effective in bringing the gospel to these structures as an institution, for the institution itself takes on this "manifold pluralism" for the sake of credibility.

2. The second point to be noted in relation to Kung's statement that the "ekklesia . . . is definitely the work of men" is to realize that the Church is not the Kingdom of God, but it bears a relationship to and responsibility for the Kingdom of God.

> The Kingdom of God is not the same as the Church. The Church is a corporate, organic society of men, dynamically united with the exalted Christ and infused with the power or dynamis of the Spirit. The Kingdom is not a society of men on earth; it remains essentially eschatological and transcendent, and its cosmic universality is wider than the limits of the Church. Nevertheless the purpose and mission of the Church are specified by its relationship and responsibility to the kingdom.[18]

As a corporate, organic society of men, the Church remains subject to certain sociological laws. The Church as a uniform institution cannot adequately meet the modern social situation. As Luckmann points out, the Church arose as a specialized institution in the complex social structure. "Fully specialized religious institutions arise only under conditions of considerable complexity in the social structure, including a heterogeneous social distribution of the world view. Such institutions cannot, therefore, express the hierarchy of meaning in the world view."[19] This is the sociological dilemma of the Church: as it becomes a specialized uni-form institution among many, it loses the possibility of leverage to

affect other institutions and their individual
members. Sociologically the polyform Church
becomes necessary.

As Cody makes clear, the power of Christ and
the dynamis of the Spirit in intimate union with
the sociological reality can bring about this
kind of change. We are able to view the Church
thus as "a dynamic community with a life history
of constantly developing order"[20] which is in
dialectical relationship with "the reality of
the human material and historical world, which
itself does not escape the action of Christ, the
Lord. . . . This means that the grace of Christ
does not reach us only interiorly. This grace also
comes visibly in many different ways, a permanent
consequence of the Incarnation."[21]   And this
grace comes not only to the individual: the visible
action of Christ in the social world is also
grace to the Church and to groups that inhere
within the Church.

As a "theological structure" we must ask
of the Church" what is it to be in the light of
the Kingdom? What is the "coming to be" of the
Church? As an "institutional structure", the
focus is on the forms the Church has assumed.
But this second, sociological question is also
an incarnational, and thus, theological inquiry:
what has been the development of the Church as
the "institutional Incarnation"? And the first,
theological question is also sociological: in
the world of institutions, how is it possible
to "bring social institutions also onto that
level where structure exists to make freedom
possible,"[22] to establish the conditions that will
make the Kingdom of God a possibility in the world
of men?

ALIENATION, COMMUNITY, CHURCH

One effect, though not a necessary one (nor
necessarily the principle one) of complex

institutionalization has been the alienation of the members of the institution. This paradox has become somewhat more prominent as institutions have tended to articulate their own justifying principles. R. R. Niebuhr believes that this alienation becomes a part of the inner experience of the individual. He explains this in <u>Experiential Religion</u>:

> This environment with its latency of many communities of believing and many worlds has been coming into existence for decades. Now that it is here, life is a repetition of births, in which our earlier bodies or experience are never quite sloughed off, and our former passions and worlds never entirely transfigured. Birth into the family is only the first, followed by births into schools, universities, and economic markets, into citizenship and its cares, war, the professional guild, or union, and the laboratory. With each birth the "tides of faith" recede from the individual. The energy of believing that shaped his former world does not affect his new companions.[23]

This estrangement is the lot, in varying degrees, of all of us in the modern environment. At the same time, there is a new "energy of believing" that tries, without total success, to integrate the individual into the new institution that he is born into, to use Niebuhr's analogy; and this energy tries to mold the individual to the institution. At the same time the individual feels an acute sense of loss of his familiar world and estrangement and alienation from the new, producing the tension of finding meaning for the multiple realities in his everyday life.

Traditionally institutional religion served to locate the individual under the sacred canopy; but we have seen that Luckmann poses a special

135

dilemma for the Church with the development of
differentiated institutions. Yet somehow the
need for both community and individuality must
be reconciled. Institutions that fail in this
regard are anti-human in proportion to their
failure; and yet it seems inevitable that society
is now filled with such institutions.

> The disintegrated and estranged
> individual is incapable of genuine community;
> "togetherness" is an invention of a
> technical age to combat loneliness and
> boredom, yet only succeeds in compounding
> them. It is in this situation that the
> Church is afforded the challenge and
> opportunity of becoming what it is in Christ
> constituted to be . . . a fellowship in
> which individuals become persons in a con-
> text of concern and acceptance.24

We have here the mandate for the Church,
but in fact no real program. The lack of program
simply reflects the dilemma of the Church as an
institution, a dilemma felt by all who have
thought about the Church in the contemporary
situation, but one that many have had difficulty
in resolving.

The alienation of the individual in the
modern social setting, his inability to enter into
meaningful community and his tendency toward
apathy have all been documented in a variety
of social and behaviorial sciences.25 How does
the Church comply with its mandate to form community in this setting? Waldo Beach specifies
some of the characteristics of a Church providing
for this kind of community. It must be a center
of love, but a love that has a special kind of
sensitivity, calling others to develop as "self"
without restraints that would hinder a true self.
It must provide a center, and so be a force for
solidarity; at the same time it must be tolerant
and allow freedom, diversity and the opportunity
to move away from this solid core.26

136

In effect, this "sensitive" Church seems to be a Church than can take many forms to accommodate the lives of many members. It is an open Church and a tolerant Church, yet at the same time strong and supportive. Finally, Beach seems to imply a further idea about the Church as a source and center of community. Preston Williams gives precision to this idea: "There is something important about this community that we need to notice. Something that is true of the Church today, namely that it does not destroy old communities and loyalties but rather permits us to transcend them."[27]

Wilfred Sheed remarks of the Church as center and source: "The Church was a constellation of practices, built around specific holy places, but also around a moveable temple, and this seemed to meet the paired psychic needs for permanence and change, dignity and recklessness." Then with a certain ruefulness and nostalgia, Sheed adds: "But the fixed temple was finished, and the flock was dispersed."[28] The religious institution is no longer this stable and stabilizing community (or is fast disappearing as such) but some community must be made available.

The community that Beach and Williams envision would allow the individual to "be born" into different institutions in the course of his biographical career and would not cause disintegration or disorder for the person, would not demand that he regard the past as dead or dead weight; rather it would ease the many parturitions, overcome the estrangements and aid in expanding the horizons of belief rather than in splintering the history of the person.

This is to suggest a multiform Church that is present in every sphere of pluralized life, not an institutional Church that exists alongside other institutions, perhaps confusing; at best, a makeshift in an incomprehensible situation; at worst, alienating those who would try to accept the message of the Church, thus becoming a victim of the same paradox that confronts the other differentiated institutions in contemporary society.

This multiform Church has already begun, not depending on any integrated theology or sociology, but simply in response to the situation in the world. We will see several examples of this, and note some of their strengths and weaknesses.

THE FORMS OF THE CHURCH TODAY

In order to understand the development of a multiform Church, we should look, first of all, at what has happened in the Churches in the last two decades in response to the disappearance of a sacred canopy. A typology with examples of these new Church forms will precede a brief statement of polity and the theological application of these forms. While not providing an exhaustive listing of the forms of the Church today, this typology establishes a basis for analyzing and categorizing new forms in the Church. The typology, rather than being strictly polar, (as distinguished from the Church-sect typology of Troeltsch), is a typology of forms on a continuum, from that most like the familiar form to the least familiar. However, the purpose of this presentation is to present the response of the Church to its altered position in Western society and to the kinds of alienations and estrangement in various institutions that have resulted from this modern social condition.

1. Extensions of the Parish or Congregation

A logical development of the traditional parish or congregational structure is its extension to a new or unfamiliar situation. This form relies on the traditional structures and Church "polities" but bends or extends them to meet new developments. Basically, the parish can be extended in two ways.

First, the parish or congregation may take on
new or non-traditional activities, or extend
traditional activities in a new way. Examples
of this abound; but two that have been prominent
in American national media are the Judson Memorial
Church in New York City and the Glide Memorial
Church in San Francisco.[29] Both Churches have
"departed" from a traditional congregation to
devise new liturgies, new services to various
groups of people, such as "hippies", homosexuals,
the elderly; and both have used their position
and publicity to address a variety of contemporary
issues. This pattern has been followed in ways
suited to different situations by many metropolitan
churches and congregations across the country.

A second way that the traditional parish has
been extended is by the formation of an amalgamated
"ecumenical" parish. Usually under the lead of
clergymen from different denominations, a new,
larger congregation is formed, embracing a large
area that might include several traditional
congregations and parishes. Usually there is a
partial surrender of autonomy to a new, larger
congregation. Examples of this, again from
the east and west coast, are the East Harlem
Protestant Parish in New York and the East
Oakland Parish in Oakland, California. These
were ways of responding to inner-city needs through
an ecumenical endeavor. At the same time, they
were a new form of parish in a situation that had
formerly produced both social and religious
alienation.

2. The Church of a Particular Service

A more radical departure in new forms and
structures of the Church has been the development
of church forms that provide a particular service
to a given population that has come into
existence in our pluralistic world. A whole
range of such ministries exists, examples being
the coffee house ministries or the street ministries
of such "night time" ministers as Don Stewart.

However I would like to point out three forms of the "church of particular service" that relate directly to three major social institutions. [30]

1. Traditionally the parish congregation has been thought of as a service to the family; but recently there has been the rise of a specialized church form that directly and exclusively serves individuals in a separated and detached way, whether as members of a family or not. The most prominent form of this church is the "apartment house ministry"[31] but there have been other ways that this form has emerged such as church-supported or -related family service agencies. It is in this exclusive connection with domestic life that we see a new form emerging that treats the family as separated from other social areas formerly under a sacred canopy.

2. The rise of a church-form related to economic institutions has probably greatest notoriety with the "worker-priest" movement in the French Catholic Church.[32]   This was an important, if mistrusted, first step in an attempt to meet modern social institutions where, as the slogan goes, "the working class was lost to the Church". In America, a variety of church structures have arisen to meet the autonomous economic institutions. A number of "industrial missions" are in evidence, most prominent being the Detroit Industrial Mission. At another level of "economic insti- tutionalization", we find groups of intellectuals, such as the European Lay Academics, and the Mukyokai in Japan, a "non-church" composed mostly of Christian intellectuals.[33]   At a level that the sophisticated would call "trivial", but which nonetheless emphasizes this point, there is the rise of the "shopping mall church", religion catering to a major form of economic activity in a consumer society.

3. There has arisen, as well, a Church involved with the political order. The Church has always been "involved" in politics; but the new develop- ment has been a Church specifically and exclusively

140

directed toward meeting the political order.
There are many examples of this, especially with
regard to bringing about change in the political
power structure.. The use of the tactics of and
even the consultation with the late Saul Alinsky
is a clear example of this. The Ecumenical
Institute in Chicago is another case where
political change became the focus of a particular
church structure.[34] This new form of the Church
has received special emphasis in Eastern European
countries. This has been stated succinctly by
Soucek:

> We can affirm without hesitation that
> human life cannot continue much longer
> unless, at critical moments, leading
> statesmen receive insights that in the
> last analysis are derived from the Sermon
> on the Mount. This should both humble
> the Church and encourage it to be more
> bold and steadfast in its message to the
> world.[35]

Quite possibly none of these new forms is
"purely" concerned with a single institution,
although the economic ones may be faily exclusive;
but these new structures have clear-cut affinities
with the autonomous and self-justifying institutions of the modern, pluralistic world. Many
different examples of "churches of particular
service" could be listed, but to attempt an
exhaustive listing does not serve my purpose here.[36]

3. New "Community Churches"

A third type of Church form that has grown
over the past decade is a new form of community,
either as a permanent complete community or as
a "congregation" that provides a new base for
ecclesial membership different from (though
not necessarily separate from) older congregations.

The most obvious form, though perhaps not as
common as the mass media would lead us to believe

141

is the religious commune or the religious community.
While this form has roots reaching back both to
monasticism and to the "radical wing" of the
Reformation, it has enjoyed renewed popularity
in the past decade. There can be no doubt that
this movement stems in great part from the socio-
cultural conditions we have been considering but
it seems to represent the desire to construct a
new "sacred canopy", an overarching system that
embraces most aspects of life. In this sense,
it surely represents a conservative reaction
to socio-cultural pluralism, whatever the outward
manifestation a religious commune might have.
It is this conservative geist that makes them akin
both theologically and sociologically to certain
manifestations in the "radical reformation".

Another example of a new style of religious
community that has enjoyed great coverage in the
media, especially religious affiliated media,
is the neo-Pentecostal movement or the charismatic
renewal movement. The charismatic groups seem
to be new kinds of congregations that depend
largely on a common religious and "pneumatic"
experience. This example represents the new style
of religious congregation that still seeks a
single integrating religious justification for
life's agencies; but membership in these groups
depends not on accepting a total way of life but
on similar life experiences, either of a religious
or of another social nature.[37]   Again this
attempt to form a new congregation seems to represent a conservative tendency, either cultural or
religious, on the part of Christians in the face
of a new social situation.

In other words, these new religious communes,
intentional religious communities, seem both
sociologically and theologically to be conservative
and traditional, perhaps at times in the best
sense of both adjectives. Instead of birth, geographical residence or adult commitment as the
basis for the congregation, similar religious
experience or common lifestyle provides a foundation
for congregational life.

4. "Rump ecclesiolas"

A final type that concludes the typologies (and is polar to the traditional historical parish or local congregation) of responses to socio-cultural pluralism are those dissident groups that have arisen within the Church because of dis-satisfaction with traditional institutional and indeed other ecclesial forms. These are generally grouped together under the broad rubric of "under-ground churches". In fact, these "underground churches" run a wide spectrum from groups devoted to an intense prayer life through those bent on liturgical innovation to those that center their activities on social action programs. While they were thought to be the pre-emption of the liberals, lately several conservative "underground churches" have developed.[38]

From two different approaches to theology, we find a view of Church life that supports this kind of _actual_ diversity in the Church. Rudolph Sohm proposed a view of the "Church" that from the beginning was to be viewed as a transcendent reality; individual communities were simply to be viewed as particular realizations of the Church, pointing beyond themselves to something that was indeed "beyond".

Hans Kung sees the Church _in_ _concreto_ as "manifestation of a catholicity that is open to the special significance of the local and regional church."[39] It is the local church, dealing with specific situations, that we have seen in the typology developed above. And a multiform Church will take on other forms bearing little resemblance to familiar institutional structures. Now we shall see if theology can accommodate what has been happening in the local and regional Church.

THE APPLICATION OF THEOLOGY

The "root question (is) whether or not the Church has a right to express inself in groupings

143

and structures the world is giving us within which we are called to mission, and indeed, where Christ, as Lord of the world, may be graciously at work."[40]   This is the problem that we must address specifically if we are to establish an ecclesiology of a multiform Church.

We have already presented a theology in Chapter 4 that points out the blurred boundaries between the Church and the world, that derives from this an incarnational and eschatological ecclesiology and that sees the Church as enriched with a variety of gifts as it continues its pilgrimage. Because this pilgrimage endures through a variety of historical and social contexts, "the Church necessarily and in accordance with its duty has to bow to the Law of history by which what was good yesterday is not good today. New epochs, the emergence and character of which are not under the Church's control, require from the Church action different from that of the past".[41] This new or different action is action that is suited to the times, suited to meet the social and cultural situation that has arisen.

The Church now has entered a new era of its existence: it can become an "infinite possibility thing",[42] an infinite possibility instrument of grace and power. Because the socio-cultural context in which modern man finds himself opens up for him a religion of infinite possibility, the Church, the religious institution, becomes an instrument of infinite possibility, of freedom and liberation. Following on the principle of the Incarnation, the Church takes on those forms and structures of the society that will further its mission, the preparation for the Kingdom of God. This "Institutional Incarnation" might be called in a kind of theological shorthand, the catholic ecclesiological principle.

At the same time, the Kingdom has not yet come and every human institution still stands under judgment of the <u>eschaton</u>. Each institution, including the variety of ecclesial institutions, must acknowledge its weakness, imperfection, and even sin. Each must undergo suffering, trial and purification to be a worthy instrument of the Kingdom. And it is the Church itself as multiform that judges not only social institutions but the Church itself. But this judgment of churchly and worldly structures by the Church is a judgment of love and not of condemnation; for the Church is judging itself in order to bring glory to its Lord, to make it the bride without spot or wrinkle which it is not yet but is meant to be. It is diversity and dissimilarity in the Church itself that is the reason for the existence of these characteristics in the Church in a pluralistic world. "This could indeed become the new identifying mark of the Church in our world, that it is composed, not of equal and like-minded men, but of dissimilar men, indeed, even of former enemies."[43] This diversity in the Church, bringing loving criticism to bear on both Church and the world, might be called, again in theological shorthand, the protestant ecclesiological principle.[44]

We can pursue this theological justification even further. The "covenanted community" theology of the believer's Church provides another perspective for a multiform ecclesiology. The Christian in this theological tradition makes a covenant with God and with his fellow-believers who share the same world-view and outlook. These are the believers who form a "gathered Church", traditionally to praise the Lord and live His gospel.[45] But it seems possible to extend this "free Church" theology to the contemporary ecclesial social situation.

It is the like-minded community of believers in the social institutions of the "world" that can and probably must constitute the Church in contemporary society. This seems to be a theological (as opposed to "merely" moral) imperative.

145

"Where two or three are gathered in my name, there am I in the midst of you." (Matt. 18:20) It seems that believers must gather in the name of the Lord to bring about the action of the Lord of history, to bring about the conditions for the advent of the Kingdom. And the promised presence of the Lord allows us to see the relationship between the "covenanted community" of like-minded believers and the institutional incarnation. The believing community as the Church of the Incarnation gathers consciously in the social institutions of the pluralistic society. The believer's Church has moved <u>into</u> the world to bring about its transformation, and in so doing reveals itself as incarnational and "catholic".

At the same time, the believing group of similar understanding and background begins to take on a responsibility for other Christians. This responsibility includes not only spiritual and material concern (although these are of evangelical importance; see Matt. 5 and 25), but also prophetic concern, that is, that other believers continue to persevere in their Christian belief. This is a responsibility not only to other Christian individual believers but to other Christian believing communities. This application of the theology of the "free churches" means that the Church as it exists in each institution in society bears the prophetic responsibility for other believing communities. Thus, a Church of the "counter-culture" may exhort a "businessman" Church about evangelical poverty, but in turn be warned by a "middle-class suburban" Church about the danger of scandalizing the "weaker brothers". Here we see that the "believer's Church" in the world is also a "Protestant" Church.

We must take the <u>reformanda</u> seriously in theology. A reforming of the Church means altered or different forms in actuality. "Ecclesiology can never simply take the <u>status quo</u> of the Church as its yardstick, still less seek to

146

justify it. On the contrary, taking once again the original message, the Gospel, as its starting point, it will do all it can to make critical evaluations, as a foundation for the reforms and renewals which the Church will always need."[46]

Yet the Church, existing in a concrete situation, must be reformed to meet that situation; that is, there must be a new and renewing appropriation of the gift of life in the Church, an appropriation conditioned by time, culture and the experience of man as an historical and social creature.

A positive re-interpretation of the "confessional" position leads along the same lines theologically as the re-interpretation of the "catholic" position in preceding paragraphs. The confessional position is an anthropological one: "Jesus is my Lord, -- or our Lord". But the substratum supporting this affirmation is always, "in this situation or in this historical context". Christ as the Logos is present in the world in every situation, informing it, re-forming it and moving it beyond itself. In the pluralistic social world, where we are so bound up with institutions, the confessional position theologically moves beyond the statement of "my personal Savior" to the affirmation: Jesus is the Savior of this cultural complex, he is Savior in this socio-cultural situation. This is still very concrete: salvation is for this situation. (It leaves open the possibility that there may, in fact, be socio-cultural situations that are not saved.) But it is an ecclesiology that transcends the confines of the small conventicle and moves to embrace the world so that the Lord of history may indeed bring about the world's transformation.

Before concluding this chapter, we will briefly look at certain other considerations of a theological anthropology in light of the sociological section of this monograph.

RELIGION AND THE PERSON

There are two "theological" functions that
a multiform Church can provide for the individual
in this pluralistic situation. The confusion
that currently exists for the person who is
religiously committed is well documented. A
more realistic ecclesiology can provide a less-
perplexing situation for the individual Christian;
but it may also contribute to the individual's
confusion if it is not given a full contextual
explanation.[47]

A multiform Church shall be able to furnish
the Christian with a base upon which to stand,
a form congenial with his present biographical
development. Such a multiform Church should
provide the believer with a sense of self and of
relationship to a particular community that promotes a structure, a system of values and a
personal wholeness and commitment which characterize
a religious person. At the same time, any Church
form must provide the valid locus for the renewal
and re-creation of person (as well as of social
structure) that is central to the Christian view
of man.

Furthermore, this religious presence generates
transcendent stress in a social institution where
the individual can develop as a religious person
together with those who share his outlook and
perspective. The individual is thus not caught
in a structure that might alienate him partially
or totally, but rather is involved in a form of
the Church that is compatible with his own life
and interests, but that bears a certain tension
with his conscious life. The religious presence
as transcendent momentum energizes a person to
move toward the "new" beyond himself as he presently is. At the same time, he is not divorced
from the rest of the Church because it is a multi-
form Church; he has merely become associated with
the form most compatible with his present biographical development. Moreover, while there is

differentiation in the structures of society, the individual need not experience his understanding of religion as separate from his social world, much less interpret it as a superimposition on society.

As a second result of a multiform Church, the individual is opened up to the possibility of the ever-new, which is one of the central themes of the Chrisitan revelation. The belief that God can break through human structures is central to a developed Biblical theology. In a multiform Church, the Christian becomes aware that God is not only breaking into his individual life but that He can enter any social strucuture or setting to bring it into the realm of gracious mercy. The modern world has been characterized as the "open situation"[48] and the Church cannot remain closed or be an institutional means of closure for the individual Christian. But social institutions have about them and their structures an element of ambiguity; it is the task of the Church to take advantage, for believers and others, of the openness of modern institutions to prepare for the entry of the divine initiative. Individual Christians must be aware of and directed toward this openness, for this is the basic condition of salvation.

> Men were not to think of objective conditions that they must try to meet, but of the active initiative of God coming to them and offereing them the Kingdom. God sought out the sinner while he was a sinner. Jesus asked, in the first place, only openness or receptivity. Such openness and receptivity, he found more frequently among those who know themselves as sinners than among the outwardly righteous members of society.[49]

Such receptivity and openness may be possible in a unique way in the institutions of the modern world. Our last consideration here will be to

examine, from the theological viewpoint, the
relationship between pluralism and "secularization".

THEOLOGY AND MODERNIZATION

Secularization is not unrelated to pluralism
as we have seen; but it is perhaps better understood as an historical process that was one of
the formative elements in modern society that
has led to pluralism. Secularization was a
process in which more particularized values replaced
a transcendent value system; it was by no means
a loss of values.

"Secularization" in its early phases
was not a process in which traditional
sacred values simply faded away. It was
a process in which autonomous institutional
"ideologies" replaced, within their own
domain, an overarching and transcendent
universe of norms.[50]

In this sense, then, even the Church went
through a process of "secularlization" which, as
we shall see in a moment, may have worked to the
advantage of religion. For we should at this
point explore the theological implications not
only of secularization but also of pluralism. It
is important to remember that secularizaton in
this view should not be opposed to religion or
even religious institutions but should be considered
as part of that complex of processes that go to
make up modernization: as such, it can help or
hinder religion and religious institutions.

As we have seen, the blurred boundary between
the Church and the world allows for the Church to
be present in human life, which is as it should be.
Human institutions, without losing any of their
humanness, have been "taken up in Christ". There
is a tension, certainly, between the "natural"
and the "supernatural", the "revelational" and
the "rational", but this does not mean that there

150

is more that one reality, God's and "the world's", and that the Church or the Christian or groups of Christians can therefore leave the world to its own devices. "The unity of the reality of God and of the world, which has been accomplished in Christ, is repeated, or more exactly, is realized ever afresh in the life of men."[51] It is this mature thought of Bonhoeffer that gives us the clues to the relationship between Church and human institutions. It is in the life of men that we see then tension and resolution of the unity of God and the world; and this resolution must be worked out again and again in man's history.

In modern society, human institutions as "secularized" are to be brought to their own fulfillment. The values they seek to realize, while not absolute, are to be sought after since the world has a fundamental, underlying unity with God. The Church becomes itself in these human institutions which are "secularized" in Luckmann's sense, but never divorced from God.

It is this search for and affirmation of values, goals and goods that is the part of the task of the Church in the "secularized" world. This is a benefit that has accrued to the Church by its own "secularization". Because of the great diversity in modern society, all institutions, including the Church, have become much more functionally specific: they perform one or a few well-defined, circumscribed functions in modern society. In this perspective,

> .....the so-called secular city is not secular in the sense that religion is no longer important, but rather in this, that the direct and specific function of religion is more limited than it was in the past. It is limited, however, to that extremely important role of constructing meaning and values for human life.[52]

This search for and construction of a meaning system is in conjunction with and part of the development of the individual's biography. But the community of believers must discriminate in the light of their evangelical faith and decide for those values which they believe promote the gospel and the Kingdom of God. Accordingly they must affirm the unity between God and the world that has been achieved in Christ, and they must affirm it anew for these times.

Thus a tension is involved in a "secularized" world; there is no random and indiscriminate sanctoning of what was, or is, as inevitable and therefore as good. Rather the Church exists to bring out the potential in the "<u>seculum</u>", the transcendent potential in the world that is the theatre of God's activity.

Yet the Church is in the world not primarily as a "pronouncer" of moral doctrine, although I do not want to discount this aspect of the Church's work.[53] The Church is involved in the secular to bring about the fullness of the Kingdom. This revelation of the "human", of freedom, of the world in union with God is what the Church is <u>to be</u> in the world.

A final significance of this tension that comes about if the Church is part of a pluralistic world is that the Church provides a way of understanding a "pluralistic universe", to use William James' phrase. Bellah agrees with this line of thought: "We must realize with Alfred Schutz that there are multiple realities and that human growth requires the ability to move easily between them and will be blocked by setting up one as a despot to tyrannize over the others."[54] It is the multiform structures of the Church that have not only developed in tension with the institutional patterns in modern society but have also provided a model for our times. This model allows individuals and institutions to comprehend the openness and receptivity that is necessary

for entry into the Kingdom. And openness allows
the creative presence of God to operate and
establish his Kingdom of justice and love. None
of this is possible by human institutions; but it
will happen in human institutions, God's theater
and domain.

CONCLUSION

     In this chapter we have been facing the specific
problem of the relationship of a theological
ecclesiology to changes both in the Church and
in society. In the previous chapter we have
examined an ecclesiology that provides an overall
basis for a multiform Church. Here in this
chapter the implications of this theology for the
Church and for believers today have been explored.
How is the Church incarnational, eschatological,
charismatic and counter-institutional in the
absence of a sacred canopy?

     It has not been necessary to expose the
many ecclesiologies that stand behind these forms
of the Church. Rather what I have been elaborating
here is a theology of many ecclesiologies, a
"meta-ecclesiology". In the perspective of this
theology, to demand rigid conformity is not only
sociologically impossible, it turns out to be
theologically difficult to defend as well. In
fact, the burden of proof is on the "conformist"
to make a case for his ecclesiology.

     However, it should be noted that this
theological view is an extension of a western
tradition. Pluriformity has not been absent;
but now under the pressure of social change it
has taken on a paramount position. H. Richard
Niebuhr noted in 1934:

          (Monasticism's) western form from the
     sixth century onward was social and
     missionary. Medieval Catholicism, however,
     was able to unite this sectarianism with

153

the ecclesiastical movement and to place
monasticism in the service of the
inclusive church.[55]

In the modern context, the theological solution offered here proposes a "catholic" or
ecclesiastical view, but of an open Church, allowing
for a "sectarian" impulse in a much fuller way,
in dynamic dialectic relationship with the society
in which the Church exists.

This is not to rule out the "denomination",
but to place the denominational form of the Church
in a different context. The denomination, in this
view, will not be the pervasive Church form of
the future and is not going to continue as the
dominant Church form in our society, "a more or
less permanent solution to the problem of the
relationship between religion and society."[56]
The denomination itself is open to the charges
that Niebuhr brought against it in the first
chapter of The Social Sources of Denominationalism,[57]
and must exist in continual tension in a social
and ecclesial context if it is not to succumb
to those dangers.[58]

Both tension and unity in the Church will
be the subject of the final chapter.

REFERENCES

1. Cox, Harvey. The Secular City. p. 116.

2. Mirgeler, Albert. Mutations of Western Christianity, trans. by Edward Quinn. Notre Dame: University of Notre Dame Press, 1968. pp. 128-129.

3. My notion of transcendence, developed before reading Huston Smith, agrees with the general lines of his typology. Cf. "The Reach and the Grasp. Transcendence Today", in Richardson, Herbert W. and Cutler, Donald R. eds.. Transcendence. Boston: Beacon Press, 1969. pp. 1-17. Distinguishing vertical from horizontal transcendence, I would describe vertical transcendence as a movement beyond "my" present state to that which is not within "my" own experience; or a being-made-new from a source of being outside the normal range of experience.

4. Arntz, Joseph, "Is There a New Openness to the Church's Charismatic Testimony?" in Metz, J. B. ed. Perspectives of a Political Ecclesiology, Concilium, Vol. 66. New York: Herder and Herder, 1971. p. 89.

5. Moltmann, Jurgen. A Theology of Hope. New York: Harper & Row, 1967. p. 307.

6. I am indebted to Yinger, J. Milton. Religion, Society and the Individual. New York: The MacMillan Company, 1957. p. 253, for this insight. However, my application is in quite a different direction than Yinger's.

7. Cf. also Luckmann, T. The Invisible Religion. P. 11.

8. Braaten, Carl F., "The Church in Ecumenical and Cultural Crossfire", p. 291.

155

9. Robin Williams, Jr. argues in <u>American</u>
    <u>Society</u>, 3d ed. New York: Borzio Books,
    1970. pp. 235-236, that in pluralistic
    America this guiding norm is agreement about
    <u>process</u> that allows order to be preserved
    in the pluralistic web of divergent and
    conflicting values.

10. MacIver, R. M. and Page, Charles. <u>Society</u>:
    <u>An</u> <u>Introductory</u> <u>Analysis</u>. New York: Holt,
    1947. p. 53.

11. Niebuhr, H. Richard. <u>The</u> <u>Social</u> <u>Sources</u>
    <u>of</u> <u>Denominationalism</u>. Cleveland: World
    Publishing Co., 1957. p. 16. (Originally
    published in 1929.)

12. Graham, Aelard. <u>The</u> <u>End</u> <u>of</u> <u>Religion</u>.
    New York: Harcourt, Brace, Jovanovich, 1971.
    p. 250.

13. Kung, Hans. <u>The</u> <u>Church</u>. New York: Sheed
    and Ward, 1967. p. 83.

14. Ibid. p. 93.

15. deAlbornoz, A. F. Carillo, "Religious
    Liberty, Human Freedom and Responsible
    Government", in Matthews, Z. K. ed.
    <u>Responsible</u> <u>Government</u> <u>in</u> <u>a</u> <u>Revolutionary</u>
    <u>Age</u>. p. 236.

16. Niebuhr, H. Richard. <u>The</u> <u>Social</u> <u>Sources</u>
    <u>of</u> <u>Denominationalism</u>. p. 24.

17. Lonergan, S.J., Bernard. <u>Doctrinal</u>
    <u>Pluralism</u>. Milwaukee: Marquette University
    Press, 1971. p. 23. Lonergan employs "pluralism"
    in a more inclusive sense.

18. Cody, O.S.B., Aelred, "Foundations of the
    Church", in <u>Theological</u> <u>Studies</u> 34:1 (March,
    1973): 13.

19. Luckmann, T. <u>The Invisible Religion</u>. p. 80.
(<u>Heterogeneous</u>, my emphasis.)

20. Prusak, Bernard P., "A Poly-Structured
Church: Primitive Reality and Present Options",
in Devine, George, ed. <u>That They May Live</u>.
Staten Island: Alba House, 1972.

21. Schillebeeckx, E., "Parole et Sacrement dans
L'Englise", <u>Lumière et Vie</u>, Tome IX:46
(Janvier-Mars, 1960). p. 34.

22. Rahner, K., "Institution and Freedom",
<u>Manuscript only</u>, p. 3.

23. Niebuhr, Richard R. <u>Experiential Religion</u>.
New York: Harper & Row, 1972. p. 67.

24. Coleman, Rt. Rev., William R., "Confronting
the Cultural Challenges", in Jefferson, Rev.,
P. C., ed. <u>The Church in the 60's</u>. Ottawa:
The Anglican Congress, 1963. p. 93.

25. A sociologist, Bryan Willson; an economist
and sociologist, Reihnard Bendix; and a
psychologist Rollo May.

Willson, Bryan. <u>Religion in Secular
Society</u>. p. 260: "Work, which ceases to
be part of a life itself with the passing
of agrarian society (that is, for farmers,)
became a <u>calling</u> and was recognized as a
distincitive activity of life, sanctified in
religious terms, and was gradually transformed
into being a <u>job</u>, supported strictly by the
institutional order and an unmediated
interest relationship."

Bendix, Reinhard, "The Comparative
Analysis of Historical Change", in Burns, Tom,
ed. <u>Social Theory and Economic Change</u>. London:
Tavistock Publications, 1967. p. 82. "The
alienation of intellectuals is a by-product of
industrialization itself, for industrialization
creates a mass public and a market for

intellectual products and thus accentuates
the elitism of some, the populism of others,
and the ambivalence of all intellectuals,
especially through their awareness of the
discrepancies between high culture and
popular culture."

May, Rollo. _Love_ and _Will_. New York:
Norton, 1969, Chapter 1, passim.

26. Cf. Beach, Waldo. Christian Community and
    American Society. Philadelphia: The
    Westminster Press, 1969. pp. 41-42.

27. Williams, Preston, "Through Conflict Comes
    New Understanding", Harvard Divinity Bulletin
    2:2 (November, 1971): 2. Text of sermon.

28. Sheed, Wilfred, "America's Catholics", The
    New York Review of Books, March 7, 1974,
    pp. 20-21. Sheed's remarks about the Catholic
    "community" are applicable, mutatis mutandis,
    to any denomination in America.

29. For Judson, see, e.g., "Report by Letty M.
    Russell", Union Seminary Quarterly Review
    21:3 (March, 1966): 333-338.

    For Glide, see, e.g., Putney, Michael,
    "The Glide Path to God", The National
    Observer. February 24, 1973, p. 1.

30. Thus Luckmann (p. 61) speaks of "clearly
    differentiated institutional areas such as
    kinship, the division of labor and the
    regulation of power". Cf. Inkeles, Alex.
    What is Sociology? Englewood Cliffs:
    Prentice Hall, 1964. p. 68; and Lundberg,
    George A., et al. Sociology, 4th ed.
    New York: Harper and Row, 1968. p. 709.

31. Goodman, Grace Ann. The Church and the
    Apartmenthouse. New York: Board of
    National Missions, United Presbyterian Church,
    U.S.A., 1966.

32. The Worker Priest: A Collective Documentation. trans. by John Petrie (pseudonym). London: Routledge and Keegan Paul, 1956.

33. Brunner, E., "A Unique Christian Mission: The Mukyokai (Non-Church) Movement in Japan", in Leibrecht, Walter, ed. Religion and Culture. Essays in Honor of Paul Tillich. New York: Harper and Brothers, 1959. pp. 287-290.

34. Meeting the political institution was not the purpose for the formation of the Institute; however, this became the "hidden agenda" of the Institute as it developed in the particular social environment.

35. Soucek, J. B., "Eastern Europe and the West in the Search for Peace", p. 111.

36. One such listing is provided in Reitz, Rudiger, The Church in Experiment, Nashville: Abingdon Press, 1969. pp. 195-198. I have used this list as one source in this section.

37. One observer who believes he discerns the combination of religious and other social experiences forming this kind of group is Michael I. Harrison. See his article, "Sources of Recruitment to Catholic Pente costalism", Journal for the Scientific Study of Religion 13:1 (March, 1974): 49-64. When this article was first presented as a paper, its title was "Sources of Recruitment to Catholic Pentecostalism, a Middle-Class Movement". (Emphasis mine.) Paper presented at the annual meeting of the Society for the Scientific Study of Religion, October, 1972.

38. Meredith McGuire's study of sixteen "underground" congregations revealed the wide range of these groups. However, she found that all of them revealed a desire to come to grips with the problems of religious beliefs in

159

our society. See Meredith McGuire, "The 'Underground Church' Movement in American Catholicism," a paper presented at the annual meeting of the Society for the Scientific Study of Religion, October, 1972; and Meredith B. McGuire, "Toward a Sociological Interpretation of the 'Underground Church' Movement," Review of Religious Research 14:1 (Fall 1972): 41-46. An earlier book edited by Malcolm Boyd, The Underground Church, rev. ed. (Baltimore: Penguin, 1969) provides a collage of descriptive material.

39. Kung, Hans. The Living Church. London: Sheed and Ward, 1965. p. 97.

40. Pennybacker, A. M., "The Question of Denominational Sovereignty", mimeographed report to the Cleveland Council of Churches, n.d., p. 1.

41. Rahner, Karl. The Christian of the Future. Montreal: Palm Publishers, 1967. p. 17.

42. Bellah, Robert N. Reyond Belief. P. 40. Bellah, in his famous essay on "Religious Evoluntion", believes that modern religion has moved beyond dualism to a multiplex world view and symbol system. I am not concerned here with his view of religious evolution; but I certainly am in agreement with the general lines of his description of modern religion.

43. Moltmann, Jurgen. Religion, Revolution and the Future. New York: Charles Scribners' Sons, 1969. p. 141. In this connection, it is interesting to note that Rahner treats the theme of "Inevitable disagreement in the Church." (Italics mine.) Subheading in the Dynamic Element in the Church. p. 73.

44. In this section, I use Tillich's terms, Catholic and Protestant principles in the general sense in which he meant "Catholic substance" and "Protestant principle". But

160

I am using them in a more generalized and
less precise sense, more evocatively than
denominatively. See The Protestant Era,
abridged edition. Chicago: University
Press, 1957; and Systematic Theology,
vol. 3. Chicago: University Press, 1963.

45. See Daniel O'Hanlon, "What Can Catholics Learn
from the Free Churchs," in Kung, Hans,
ed. Do We Know The Others? Concilium, Vol. 14.
New York: Paulist Press, 1966. p. 98.

46. Kung, Hans. The Church. p. 28.

47. Obviously, this monograph is not concerned
with a fully developed theological anthropology,
but some hints in the direction of such an
anthropology have already been indicated and
some other elements are presented here.

48. vonOppen, Dietrich, "Man in the Open Situation",
in Funk, Robert W. ed. Journal for Theology
and Church, Vol. 2. Translating Theology into
the Modern Age. New York: Harper & Row, 1965.
pp. 130-158.

49. Cobb, John B. The Structure of Christian
Existence. Philadelphia: Westminster Press,
1967. p. 115.

50. Luckmann, Thomas. The Invisible Religion. p. 101.

51. Bonhoeffer, Dietrich. Eberhard Bethge, ed.
Ethics. New York: The MacMillan Company, 1965.
pp. 198-199. This paragraph utilizes the
thought of Bonhoeffer in his reflection on the
Church.

52. Greeley, A. The Hesitant Pilgrim. American
Catholicism after the Council. Garden City:
Doubleday Image Books, 1969. p. 62. Greeley
is here popularizing a thesis developed by
Parsons in an imporatant essay, "Christianity
and Modern Industrial Society", in
Tiryakian, Edward A., ed. Sociological

is not necessarily irreligious; and the modern Christian can bring the Church into being in contemporary social institutions in conjunction with other believers. In the following chapter, I shall present this idea relying especially on Thomas Luckmann's discussion of the "myth of secularization".

CHAPTER 6

AGELESS CHURCH: MODERN IN THE MODERN WORLD.

We have been reviewing the elements that
constitute a new situation in the modern world.
Pluralization distinguishes the modern world
from other forms of social life that mankind has
experienced in the past. Thus we can say that
the process of pluralization and the resultant
institutional pluralism that we have been
considering is one of the marks of the modern
world, along with urbanization, industrialization
and bureaucratization. In fact, it seems that
pluralization is intimately connected with the
other three modernizing processes; but we cannot pursue this point further here.

If in one sense this situation is new, in
another sense it is newly born but has been
coming into existence over a long span of history;
surely it is part of the upheaval and development of decades and even centuries. Already
in the Enlightenment "this problematic situation"
concerning religion arose. Enlightenment criticism
sought to expose religion as a separate institution
"based on a specific social practice and power
structure".[1] Thus the criticism of religion,
at least of religious institutions, as "superstructure" began early enough in the modern era,
a criticism designed to discredit religion, but
in fact indicating the development of many
institutions no longer tied in with "Christendom"
as an all-embracing socio-religious symbol.

HISTORICAL CONSCIOUSNESS AND THE SELF-UNDERSTANDING OF THE CHURCH

What began with the Enlightenment and continued throughout the nineteenth century was the

development of a new self-understanding on the part of man. This new self-understanding can be understood by the general rubric of "historical consciousness". In a general way, historical consciousness means an understanding of the self, as individual self or social self, singular self or plural self, as existing in a continuum having a past and evolving toward a future which while conditioned by the past may be different than either past or present. Most analysts believe that the rise of historical consciousness on the part of a large number of people is specific to the modern age and to modern man.

Certainly this generalized description of historical consciousness does not exhaust the meaning of the phrase; and in fact, its significance hinges on several factors: it does in fact mean many things. But in the context of understanding the Church, it refers with particular emphasis to two aspects of the Church that can be seen as specifically modern and difficult if not impossible of realization except in the modern world.

First, historical consciousness has allowed modern man to see the social and cultural relativism of his own situation. The results of this for the Church meant, for most of the 19th century, a view of the Church as a relativistic phenomenon. What has become possible for us now, with a somewhat wider perspective and keener perception of the situation, is a distinction and understanding of the relativistic aspects of the ecclesia without losing sight of the elements of enduring permanence. What both liberal Protestant scholarship of the 19th century and Pio Nono were affirming were true; but neither can be taken as exclusive statements. •

Theologically we can now see the Church as capable of fitting into many cultural contexts, and what is critical in my analysis, of fitting into many cultural contexts simultaneously and

164

in juxtaposition. In a pluralistic society there are indeed many "cultural" contexts juxtaposed to each other for each institution in society is busy creating a "culture" of its own. It is precisely this pluralistically cultural situation that the Church must meet; and in understanding its own historical relativity it will be able to meet this pluralism. Rahner has warned that "even in the Church human strata coexist chronologically which sociologically, intellectually and culturally belong to quite different epochs".[2] This co-existence is not only chronological; it is geographical and local as well.

The second important feature about the rise of historical consciousness in the modern world is that historical consciousness now allows man to consciously create his own destiny. Meyer maintains that this means "man is the <u>immediate</u> maker of his world".[3] For a systematic ecclesiology, this means that the people of the Church -- the "called" -- are called to this vocation: to assemble <u>consciously</u> in the style, mode and manner that expresses their relationship to God. This conscious coming together is not only cultic but cultural. As conscious, self-conscious if you wish, and cultural, such a gathering must be expressive of the life-meaning of those gathered. It cannot be trivial or alien. But it is precisely diversity that is demanded if the Church is not to be alien to many in a pluralized world. Believers must create an assembly of the called that expresses their own individual and social reality.

Now, while the assembly of those who regarded themselves as called or elect frequently did just that in the past, they did not do it in this self-conscious fashion, in self-awareness of the creation of their own destiny. Indeed, the justification of the creation of a new "ecclesial community" has most often been a harkening back to a vision of the primitive Church. Historical consciousness allows us to develop a vision of

165

the Church that can meet the future because it is always at the disposal of both God and man; and so the Church is always seen as relative both in its historical and eschatological dimensions.

While historical consciousness makes this new view possible, it is sociology that provides the empirical data that can be checked and interpreted. Sociology then permits this new style of ecclesial self-understanding to take on concrete form in this self-conscious, self-directive way. The sociological analysis of the situation in which the Church finds itself and must now consciously take on concrete form is based on this historical consciousness but also challenges the theologian to test his theology against empirical evidence. This is the new direction in which theology has moved; and the direction we have pursued here in examining ecclesiological reality.

In this investigation there have been three areas of consideration that have seemed important for our purposes. The ecclesiology that has been presented here considers an anthropology, the question of religion, and the nature of the Church. Obviously, conclusions about these three areas will be specific in terms of this investigation; this is not a full-blown theology of man, or religion or of the Church.

ANTHROPOLOGY AND PLURALISM

Several important ideas come to the fore with regard to the person and the Church in a pluralistic society. The individual person is no longer "tied down" to a specific denomination. As a member of the Church, the person identifies with Christianity; but in the course of his or her biographical career, the person can and probably will move from one form of the Church to another, depending on the social instititutions that are imporatnt at a particular stage in the person's life. The individual lives in the open situation, and the Church must also be an open Church, as we shall see.

This view of man who is open to new ecclesial experiences corresponds to the "psycho-historical" view of man proposed by Robert J. Lifton, which he calls "Protean Man".[4] Briefly, we may summarize Lifton's conception of Protean man with three characteristics, although "characteristic" does not convey the fluidity or process that underlies this emerging personality-type. First, Protean man is involved in his own "continuous psychic re-creation".[5] By this, Lifton means that such a person is continuously altering his own sense of self: a changing self in a changing world seems to be the model here. In particular, the ability to change in certain areas of one's personality seems to promote the chances for healthy survival in a world of "historical dis-location"[6] (that dramatic social change brought about by contemporary historical processes).

Secondly, and related to this psychic re-creation, is a "series of experiments and explora-tions"[7] upon which Protean man or woman embarks. The Protean style includes the willingness and openness to experiment with and to explore the multiplex realities open to man today when he consciously faces his changing milieu. The dead weight of biography and culture cannot impede the individual from exploring new social areas of significance.

Finally, Lifton sees developing in this new personality type a pattern of shifting allegiances and commitments[8] that will allow Protean man to alter previous convictions, all the while retaining a certain constancy, especially anti-cipation of experiment and the experience of change itself.[9] This Protean personality seems most likely to be open to and to experiment with new modes of transcendence in a pluralistic universe.

167

It is this Protean Man who is not uncommitted, but not so rigid as to remain unchanging not only in a changing world but in his own changing situation as he moves into and through a number of worlds in the course of his life-career. As Lifton believes that Protean man is the characteriological type that will survive,[10] so it seems safe to say that Protean Christian is the religious type will survive, at least in our era.

A further consideration arises at this point. Is it possible for the Protean and pluralized Christian to enter into any true relationship with others who do not simultaneously share his commitments or world view? This is a crucial question for both an ethical system[11] and for "missiology". A fully developed answer is not possible here; but we may gain some insights from the phenomenological sociology of Alfred Schutz and his followers.[12]

Schutz points out that phenomenologically the individual who has learned to deal with multiple realities can stand outside of these realities and in fact is able to resonate with the world view of these realities that are not "thematized" in his everyday, working world.

This seems to be a description of the subjective aspect of religion, that sense of transcendence which is the ability to stand outside oneself. This rough description of transcendence does not specify the differences between this-worldly, horizontal transcendence and other-worldly, vertical transcendence; but it gives us a clue to facing the anthropological problem posed by pluralism. The "pluralized" Christian, the person who has moved successfully if not always easily into the multi-forms of the Church, is precisely the one who will in fact have the ability to relate to others who do not in fact share the present world-view of the Protean Christian, for this is precisely the person who has "been born" into different realities and has experienced living in different everyday worlds.

This issue of transcendence, the ability to stand outside oneself, speaks of the nature of religion and raises the question of the nature and meaning of religion in the modern world.

THE NATURE OF RELIGION IN A PLURALISTIC SOCIETY

The question of the nature of religion is discussed and debated by theologians, historians, sociologists, anthropologists and psychologists. The literature is immense and of course, the issues here are not about the nature of religion at all, but about the understanding and concept of the Church. However, a consideration of pluralism allows us to comment on the "nature of religion" as it appears in the modern world. Certainly pluralism as it has affected religion gives us some insights into the religious situation; and a comment about religion seems necessary, since the Church, sociologically, has been the dominant religious institution in our society, and hence its pre-eminent expression.

First what we have been describing as pluralism might be confused with secularism, or be seen as synonymous with secularism. On this score, it is important to note once again that not all observers agree that secularism has occurred. Among sociologists, Parsons is not convinced about the arguments for secularism. He believes that religion has "lost many functions"[13] that we might have associated with earlier forms of religion (he calls them "previous religious types"), but that religion is not less important nor in fact less influential in the ordinary affairs of people. The institutionalization, Parson argues, is indeed different, partly due to denominationalism and partly due to the emphasis on autonomy; but in effect his argument is that we must not mistake the form for the substance. While we have not entered a religious millenium, the modern world is not less religious than earlier times, and in fact, might be even more religious.

Luckmann argues similarly in both The Invisible Religion[14] and in "Secularization: A Contemporary Myth".[15] In The Invisible Religion, the case is made for the shift of religion from the puble sphere to private life, a "privatization" of religion. But this does not leave the public sphere, or secondary institutions, "religionless" or secular. Rather when people as religious individuals work or act in these secondard institutions, they do not divorce their religious commitments from their everyday activity. Rather they bring these religious values and religious world-view to the public arena; but this is a religious system that has been formed privately and by a diversified and separate institution, the religious institution, in a highly diversified society. Institutional diversification has not meant the end of religion; but its "public" position is in a diversified institution.[16]

This argument is re-presented and expanded in the essay, "Secularization: A Contemporary Myth". There, Luckmann makes the point that to the "objective, outside observer" of modern institutions, that is, the sociologist or anthropologist, they may appear to be secularized. But in fact from the insider, from the point of view of the participants, they are in fact not secularized at all. The individuals who make up these institutions bring a value-system, a world view and a sense of transcendence to these institutions. It should be noted that this system of privatized religion does not harmonize necessarily with the "autonomous" system of the institutions of social action. But Luckmann's point is that social actors do not enter into social institutions without their own "religious system", albeit a privatized one.

170

This contention of Luckmann dovetails with the point of view expressed here, that the Church can and in fact does come into being in a new way in the institutions of modern society. Our question has been the recognition of the Church's presence.[17]

The point is that pluralism is not necessarily secularism because it is possible, and in fact these analysts believe, very likely, that religion has not vanished from the public scene but appears in a different form. The problem for the contemporary Christian is an ethnocentric view of religion. He expects religion to look like "his religion", to take on the shapes, forms and institutional patterns that he is accustomed to. This narrower view of religion misses the point of view of the gospels, that religion, relationship to God is not confined to the ways that men have devised in the past (cf. John 4:21 fl.) nor to the patterns and observances that have become the "accepted pattern". In fact, it is this confusion of the nature of religion with the forms of religion that has led to disastrous consequences for the Church in many of her endeavors.

The task for Christians in a diversified and pluralistic world is not to deplore a "false" secularization, nor to huddle in a ghettoized Church but to bring the Church into being, consciously and intentionally, in the diversified institutions of the modern world. This is not to hearken back to some idealized union of "religion and society", much less to make "faith" somehow the norm or guide for "secular" (i.e., of and in the world) institutions. Rather as we have already seen, the Church is to be active to bring the world and its institutions to God's Kingdom. This is why a multi-form Church becomes a necessity in our age.

This question of the "myth of secularization" leads into a second observation about the nature of religion, especially in the contemporary world.

Religion seems to be undergoing a process not of
de-institutionalization, but rather, and here
I depart from Luckmann's analysis, of re-institutionalization. This process has been pointed
out in the so-called "underdeveloped" countries,
and extensive analysis has been presented of
Africa[18] and Latin America[19] concerning new
religious institutions. Less attention has been
paid to such re-institutionalization in "developed"
societies, except as it appears in more exotic
or even bizarre forms. But it is this process
of re-institutionalization for itself that the
Church must face.

For a "study aspect of this theological
endeavor"[20] the Church must develop a critique
of itself and of its failure to meet many issues
and areas of modern society. It must then,
still as part of a "study aspect", search in the
theological resources to understand better what
it is that the Church itself is supposed to be and
to do. This has been suggested, at least, here
in Chapter 4. This effort can be aided by close
examination of the analysis of behaviorial and
social sciences. But the Church must also search
in her own resources to understand the nature of
religion for modern society.

However, in conjunction with and operating
at the same time as this "study aspect", there
is also the practical theological aspect which
cannot wait until a full-study is completed.
It cannot wait, because, first, the Church must
make every effort to act in the world, it cannot withdraw until it is certain of what it must
do. Salvation takes place in the world of men
and their institutions. And because, secondly,
the Church must remain in constant dialogue
with the world in order better to understand,
reflect and act.

If the Church undertakes this theological
endeavor, a re-institutionalization process will
follow inevitably. At the same time, this

re-institutionalization will itself be subject
to criticism in ways we have suggested. It is
the multi-form Church that is best able to be the
"conscience" of the institutions, much as the
various denominations have in the past and in
the present exercised this "conscience function"
for each other, albeit unconsciously and
unwittingly at times.

The issue of "conscious conscience", con-
sciousness-raising or constienticizao on the part
of the Church raises another issue about the nature
of religion. Sociologists of religion point out,
rightly, that one of the traditional functions
of religion in society has been to integrate the
society, to bring about a special cohesion in the
society to provide for its continuance and
stability.[21] The re-institutionalization of
religion provides, at the theoretical level, the
basis for reasserting this function in society.
In their dialogic confrontation with each other,
the multi-forms resulting from this re-institutionalization can certainly provide a cohesive
center of unity not only for themselves but also
for the society.

Because this multi-form Church comes into
existence in the institutions of society, it
provides the basis of unity as well as of prophetic
criticism of the society. The two, of course,
are not unrelated. Such a Church would be like
a net-work or a web extending through the society
and binding it together. At the same time, by
the very fact of being in critical dialogue with
modern society, it binds modern society together
and co-inheres in the society in a kind of dialectic
relationship. Here we are moving beyond the
question of religion and society, however, and
are facing the issue of the nature of the Church,
its function in society and the possiblity of
the unity of a multi-form Church.

Sociology has brought about a re-examination of the structure of the Church, not only in regard to socio-cultural pluralism, the specific issue here, but more generally as well. Peter Berger maintains that this relativizing is one of the fruits of Sociology[23] and as such is to be applauded. When seen in this relative perspective, the Church is not confined to one sociological form, nor in fact to a limited number of such forms. Rather this "new" science has opened up the possibility of a multi-form Church.

1. Structural Nature of the Church

Troeltsch was already indicating something of this order when he wrote:

> A situation in which different churches
> can exist side by side will only become
> possible when a different conception of
> truth prevails; this was, indeed, the
> case in pre-Catholic Christianity,
> whose great variety was connected with
> a conception of truth which involved an
> individualistic "enthusiasm".[24]

It is important in understanding the approach here that Troeltsch does not talk of relative truth, but different conceptions of truth. The impact of historical consciousness coupled with socio-logical methodology does not necessarily imply a relativizing of reality, but rather has opened up the relative aspects of reality, including religious reality and the Church. This kind of "relativizing" has allowed "different Churches" to begin to exist side by side. We must be open to a theology of these relative aspects of the Church.

This gives rise to a concept of the Church as the "open Church". The multi-form Church does not lock individuals into a particlar structure, nor is the Church itself locked into structures, even a plurality of structures. The Church thus has the nature not only of a voluntary association, but of a free and open voluntary association. Individuals are able to and in fact encouraged to move from one ecclesial form to another as they themselves change or as they experience social change in their own milieu. Thus as individuals move through their biographical career, they may seek out those forms of the Church that not only meet their needs but also provide them with the community that is the basis for their religious experience.[25]

At the same time that the individual changes, he or she also experiences social change in the environing world. This external change also may influence individuals to seek another form of religion, one that is present in and for a new situation. (It may also have the effect of making them seek the familiar, hence a multi-form Church, balancing permanent and relative, social and religious factors.) The Church must be found by those who seek it in the variety of diversified institutions in the contemporary world. Thus,

> An ekklesia is not something that is formed and founded once and for all and remains unchanged; it becomes an ekklesia by the fact of a separated concrete event, people coming together and congregating, in particular congregating for the purpose of worshipping God.[26]

It is this congregation of people -- congregation in the active sense of congregating -- in an historical time and place that is the multi-form Church, for the congregation can occur anywhere, in nearly any social situation.

It is important to note, in discussing the
nature of the Church, that the emphasis on such a
broad anthropological base does not presume a
limitation on divine power; that can reach through
any structure. But will individuals be open to
the transcending reality, will they be attracted
to religion and recognize the presence and power
of the divine in a diversified and pluralistic
social milieu, if the Church is not diversified
and multi-form, capable of being understood by
contemporary man? It would seem that a church
that was sociologically and theologically open
would also have for its members those who were
religiously open as well. This would seem to be
a consequence of the praxis of an incarnational
religion.

This, then, would seem to be what is theologically new in this consideration. The Church
is not only sociologically open and diverse; it
is theologically pluralistic, open and multi-
form. "As for the peoples of the earth", writes
Yves Congar, "inasmuch as they are conditioned
by a certain special way of being and possess their
own values of culture or humanity, all these
plainly have a place in the catholicity of the
Poeple of God or of the Church."[27] The "way of
being" that conditions people is not only their
location in some civilization or culture, it is
their daily activity in the social institutions
that make up such an important part of every
individual's life. This must also be incorporated
in a church truly catholic.

A concrete example of this diversity in
praxis has to do with the pluriformity of the
Catholic Church in Downtown Amsterdam, the Nether-
lands.[28] The twelve Catholic churches, formerly
separate parishes, in central Amsterdam have
each taken on specialized work, one for the youth,
another for the elderly, another concerned with
liturgical development, education, the business
community and so on. This diversification is not
only for practical purposes, nor is it merely,

176

although partially based on sociological considerations.
It is also an attempt to deal theologically with a
new situation, new at least in the sense that the
Church hadn't faced up to it adequately before.
It is a theological expression of a new form of
Church which is indeed multiform.

2. Functional Nature of the Church

    This Dutch example leads us to the function
of the Church, not in the sociological sense,
although this cannot be excluded, but in the
theological sense. This example leads to the view
of the Church as the servant Church, a popular view
today. The Church considered as servant is to
provide for the needs of the people, suffer like
the suffering servant (cf. Is. 42:1-4, 49:1-7, 50:
4-11; 52:13-53; 12 and Acts 3:13, 26; 4:27, 30) and
to serve both Christians and the world at the many
levels of "need" in the contemporary situation.
This is certainly an incarnational view of the
Church, and one that is important for the credibility
of the Church to believers and to others. Cox maintains that this service function "really refers to
the act of healing and reconciling, binding up
wounds and bridging chasms, restoring health to the
organism".[29]

    Cox, however, does not specifically refer
to the cost to or the posture of the Church. In
some way and at some level, the Church will have
to pay for this kind of service; the healing and
binding and restoring can only be accomplished at
some cost, at times tremendous cost, to the Church.
At the same time, the Church must enter into an
identity with those who are served. If chasms
are to be bridged, the Church must be on both
sides involved in the bridge-building. This
sense of suffering-servant Church has been
examined by Black theologians in particular,[30]
and they and other theologians have emphasized
the need for the Church to identify especially
with the suffering, material, social, psycho-

177

logical and spiritual, in the modern world. What must be further emphasized when discussing the necessity of identification is that the Church must work for identity on all sides, for the Church is the servant of all.

A second theological function flows from this: the prophetic activity of the Church. The Church enters into every realm of society not only to serve, console and heal; the Church is not to be easily accomodated to any social group. The Church as present and active in the social order is critical of that social order and of each segment or institution in a pluralistic society because none have as yet been freed of either individual or group selfishness and egotism. This prophetic task in a multi-form Church is operative in two ways. Just as social groups are often critical of each other, so the Church as it takes form in one social group may in prophetic candor be critical of another social group or institution, or of the Church in other areas of modern life. Beyond this, the Church in any form must never fall into the complacency that overlooks the semper reformanda but must in fact exercise a judgmental control over its own activities and its own milieu. Thus, the Church is also prophetically active in the social institutions in which it has become "incarnational".

This points up another activity of the Church, the third theological function, the proleptic. The Church exists not merely for the present but also for the future. The Church has as its task to prepare for the future, for what in faith it knows is going to happen. We have already seen that the Church is to be the instrument of bringing to fulfillment not only individuals but social groups as well. And it is in understanding this as "a corporate not merely an individual task"[31] that we see the relationship of the Church to the diversified institutions of modern society.

This function makes clear why the Church is a community. It is in its communal and corporate structure that the Church is able to participate in Christ's work of bringing about the Kingdom of God, the fullness of the created order which includes human, created institutions.

3. The Cohesive Nature of the Church

To speak of the Church as a community is to introduce the question of the unity of the Church and of the correlative function, cohesion of society including ecclesial society. Is a multi-form Church so diverse as to blur the unity of the Church and concomittantly make it in fact impossible for it to fulfill its mission in the created order, which is analogous to the socio-logical function of cohesion, i.e., bringing created order to fulness in Christ?

The question of unity is a perplexing one; but there seems to be a growing consensus among theologians that Church unity is not something "given", but instead, involves a search and partakes of a process.[32] This unity is related to a quest, a quest, which like the search for the Kingdom, must go through the world - the oikumene. The multi-form Church makes this search for unity through the world realistic, for its seems that in a multi-form Church in our society institutional religion will move through the world. Moltmann indicates his agreement with this point of view:

> The Church is not here for itself. It is here for the Kingdom of God and the freedom of the children of God; and in this sense it is here for the world. Christianity is not here for itself, but for the coming of man's true humanity, which he can and should discover through Christ and in faith. Therefore, the Church . . . must be primarily concerned with the humanity of man and the humanizing of the social order.[33]

179

So if the Church is to go through the world for the sake of the world, it must have a realistic cohesion in the world. It is this coherence in the world that is the first step toward bringing about a complete "humanizing of the social order", a function that surely is a condition for the advent of the Kingdom. But it is the coherence itself in this active and dialectical sense that leads to ecclesiological unity. For this unity is dependent, not on external imposition, but on organic development toward a fuller realization of the Church.

At the same time, Christians themselves will become more aware of their own Christian communality in both a passive and active sense, and will consciously realize ecclesiological union. Personally as well, individual Christians will enter into different forms of the Church depending on their own development; and this movement through the different forms of the one Church will increase the sense of the oneness of the Church in its manifold forms.

The sociological problem for any institution in the modern setting is to maintain diversity, to avoid stultifying uniformity. The theological field that this sociological insight reveals and to which it corresponds is that of diversification and freedom in the Church, the provisions for an area where the Spirit may blow where he wills (cf. John 3:8) and the avoidance of suffocating uniformity for those who believe according to their own socio-cultural position. The real theological problem is to maintain diversity in unity rather than vice-versa.

The tensions that exist in the theological and pastoral search for unity are a recognition of this theological problem. Consciously or unconsciously in the Church, Christians realize the need for diversity and the theological provision for diversity in the Christian tradition. Without discounting stubbornness and selfishness, it is possible to maintain that present tensions among Christian groups are a healthy attempt to prevent deadening uniformity. That tensions can be healthy has long been recognized; here it is necessary to maintain that the tension that supports and protects diversity is theologically necessary. This tension keeps open the freedom of the Church, and at the same time stands as a sign to the world that institutions cannot require of nor program uniformity into their membership.

In fact, tensions exist and presuppose some kind of unity, either structural or conceptual. Because tensions exist, it is theologically possible to talk of the already existing unity of the Church. There is a fundamental relation- ship that makes tension possible; and this relation- ship is a reality that binds Christians and Christian groups to each other in spite of many and sometimes deep differences. This tension then is a two-edged sword: it provides for diversity and at the same time presents the danger of division. Diversity is theologically and socio- logically necessary; division can be theologically and sociologically disastrous.

Thus there is no easy answer for the theological difficulties presented by this aspect of the Church: cohesion and unity in a pluralistic society. But there have never been easy answers to this issue.

We can predict that certain aspects of this difficulty will resolve themselves as present denominational structures become multi-form and similar "forms" "unite" across denominational divisions with one another. However, this will almost certainly raise new problems of unity and diversity and the old tensions will take on new forms. We must be prepared for this even as we see signs of a solution to some of the present problems of divisiveness in the Church.34

CONCLUSION

The concern of this chapter brings us up against the issue of the self-understanding of the Church. Can the Church maintain her own self-hood in a totally changed cultural situation. This is the question that confronted the 19th century theologians, and their answer was in general, "No". The Church had in fact become the Church and was no longer what Christ had in mind. The movement from primitive Christianity to early Catholicism was the end of Jesus' Christianity; this was in fact the loss of self-hood because of an altered socio-cultural situation -- Christianity moved into the Hellenistic world and became the Church. This was the verdict of nineteenth century historical criticism.

Now we have an altered view of the self-understanding of the Church. The Church or assembly (qahal) was able to maintain a continuous sense of self, even though both the socio-cultural situation was altered and the understanding of the meaning of Jesus' resurrection and glorification became ambiguous for it. If these events were not the termination of history, what then of the assembly of believers? The Church was able to come to a deeper self-understanding in the face of these crises. But this deep self-understanding did not exhaust the meaning of the Church for the world.

Once again the Church faces a rapidly changing socio-cultural situation, although not one of its own choosing. But through its own self-understanding, it should now have learned by reflection on its own past. It is the faith leading to witness that preserves the integrity of the Church. Its own self-understanding can lead it now to accept many forms and in fact a "protean form". Just as Lifton proposes "Protean man" as the characterological type that will survive, and as the "Protean believer" is the Christian who will survive as believer, so we must see the "Protean Church" as the ecclesial type that will survive in the socio-cultural situation that history's Lord has presented us with.

182

REFERENCES

1. Metz, Johannes B., "The Church's Social Function in the Light of a 'Political Theology'", in Faith and the World of Politics, Concilium, Vol. 36. Metz, Johannes B., ed. New York: Paulist Press, 1968. p. 3.

2. Rahner, Karl. The Christian of the Future. (Previously cited.) p. 18.

3. Meyer, Ben. The Church in Three Tenses. (Previously cited. Italics added.) p. 118.

4. Lifton, Robert Jay. History and Human Survival. New York: Vintage Books, 1971. pp. 311-331. This essay on Protean Man first became available in America in Partisan Review, (Winter, 1968) pp. 13-27.

5. Ibid., p. 316.

6. Ibid., p. 318.

7. Ibid., p. 319.

8. Ibid., p. 324.

9. Cf. Ibid., p. 313. From pp. 311-315 in History and Human Survival, Lifton prefaces his essay with a clarification of his idea of this characterological type and defends himself against his critics.

10. Ibid., p. 331.

11. Cf. Niebuhr, H. Richard, "The Center of Values", in Radical Monotheism and Western Culture. New York: Harper and Brothers, 1960. pp. 100-113.

12. Cf. especially Schutz, Alfred. Collected Papers, Vol. I, (previously cited); and Berger, Peter and Luckmann, T. The Social Construction of Reality. New York: Doubleday Anchor, 1967.

13. Parsons, Talcott, "Christianity and Modern Industrial Society", (previously cited). p. 67. It should be noted that Parsons' use of the term "functions" refers to a technical sociological sense, and Parsons has added his own nuance to his usage.

14. Cf., Luckmann, Thomas. The Invisible Religion. (Previously cited.)

15. Cf. Luckmann, Thomas, "Secularization: A Contemporary Myth". Unpublished paper, 1970. Luckmann, in private conversation, pointed out also that his position is very close to Robert Bellah's in "Religious Evolution".

16. Luckmann and Peter Berger maintain that religion is part of the "anthropological condition" of man, that is, that he cannot escape being religious. Only we must be insightful in discovering its manifestations.

17. Andrew Greeley is at pains to make a similar point in Unsecular Man. New York: Schocken, 1972. I believe that Parsons' and Luckmann's presentations are somewhat more sophisticated (indeed, Greeley leans heavily on Parsons) and so I have chosen to summarize them here.

18. Cf., e.g., Barrett, David B. Schism and Renewal in Africa. An analysis of six thousand contemporary religious movements. Nairobi: Oxford University Press, 1968.

19. Cf., e.g., Willems, Emilio, "Religioser Pluralismus und Klassenstruktur in Brasilien und Chile", in International Yearbook for

the Sociology of Religion, Vol. I. Koln:
Westdeutscher Verlag, 1965, pp. 190-209,
and also, Willems, Elilio. Followers of
the New Faith: Cultural Change and the
Rise of Protestantism in Brazil and Chile.
Nashville: University of Vanderbilt Press,
1967.

20. Elliot, Charles, "An Esoteric Critique of
Cartigny", in In Search of a Theology of
Development. Geneva: Committee on Society,
Development and Peace, 1969. p. 13.
Elliot makes the distinction in the theo-
logical endeavor between "study aspects"
and "activist aspects".

21. Cf. O'Dea, Thomas. The Sociology of Religion.
Englewood Cliffs: Prentice Hall, 1966, for
a good, brief presentation of this idea.

22. The choice of the title for this section is
deliberate. What is the direction the
Church should take after Vatican II and Upsala,
1968? Hopefully, this section seeks to offer
some insights into this question.

23. Berger, Peter. Invitation to Sociology. A
Humanistic Perspective. Garden City: Doubleday Anchor, 1963. pp. 48-52.

24. Troeltsch, Ernst. The Social Teaching of the
Christian Churches, Vol. I. New York: Harper
Torchbook, 1960. p. 95. Needless to say, I
do not agree with the Harnackian assumption
in this quotation; but historical scholarship has altered our conception of early
Christianity without invalidating Troeltsch's
general thesis.

25. Cf., e.g., Erik Erikson on the different
stages of development in an individual's
career and by implication, the differences
that would be necessary for an individual
to experience the transcedent. A good

treatment is in Erikson's Identity: Youth and Crisis, Chap. III, "The Life Cycle: Epigenesis of Identity". New York: Norton, 1968. pp. 91-141.

26. Kung, Hans. The Church. (Previously cited.) p. 84.

27. Congar, Yves, O.P., "The Church: The People of God" in The Church and Mankind, Concilium, Vol. I. (Previously cited.) p. 26.

28. This material is from a personal conversation with the director of Moses and Aaron Church in Amsterdam, which is dedicated to the youth work of the central city, and to education.

29. Cox, Harvey. The Secular City. (Previously cited.) p. 114.

30. Cf., e.g., Cone, James H. Black Theology and Black Power. New York: Seabury, 1969, and A Black Theology of Liberation. Philadelphia: Lippincott, 1970; or King, Martin Luther Jr. Trumpet of Conscience. New York: Harper & Row, 1968. See also Richardson, Herbert, "Martin Luther King - Unsung Theologian", in Commonweal, Vol. 88:7 (May 3, 1968) pp. 201-203. Even the novelist James Baldwin has this as one of his concerns. Cullmann develops the Christology of the "Suffering Servant" in Chapter 3, Christology of the New Testament. Philadelphia: The Westminister Press, 1959.

31. "The Quest for Structure of Missionary Congregations" An interim report of the Department on Studies in Evangelism, 1965, World Council of Churches. (Mimeo. Harvard Divinity School.) p. 6.

32. Cf. Kerkhofs, Jan, "Pluralism, Polarisation, and Communication in the Church - Some Theological Aspects", _Pro Mundi Vita_, No. 45 (1973) p. 4.

33. Moltmann, Jurgen. _Religion, Revolution and the Future_. (Previously cited.) p. 120.

34. Sociological theory recognizes this in the distinction between "manifest and latent functions", latent functions being the unintended and unanticipated consequences of any "social action". Cr. Merton, Robert K. _Social Theory and Social Structure_. 1968 enlarged edition. New York: The Free Press, 1968. pp. 73-138.

CONCLUSION

This monograph has focused on the relationship between a particular "event" in society and the impact of this event on an area of theology: the pluralization of social institutions in relationship to the religious social institution. I have tried to document the emergence of one form of socio-cultural pluralism, the form I consider most significant for the "everyday, working world", and have shown the repercussions this is having not only on the forms of institutional religion but on ecclesiology as such. We have an altered, or perhaps better, a deepened understanding of the Church because of her encounter with the world.

In this monograph the issue has been pluralism; but pluralism can refer to different things in this context.

1. Theological pluralism.

The same "truth" as received in revelation can be explained or systematized differently in different historical and cultural milieus. Thus Augustine develops a theology based on the distinction of res and signa; Aquinas refashions theology borrowing "realist" concepts, "being, nature and physics"; and Schliermacher establishes a "romantic" theology based on an awareness or feeling of absolute dependence which is irreducible to thought or will. Yet all are attempting to be faithful to the revealed Christian tradition; each is a valid, albeit incomplete, expression of the tradition.

This monograph has been an exercise in theological pluralism, but only insofar as I have attempted to systematize for our socio-cultural milieu an ecclesiology accepting the revelational experience of the Church as

189

foundational. Thus I have not attempted to present a theologically pluralistic ecclesiology in the strictest or fullest sense of theological pluralism.

2. Religious pluralism.

Religious pluralism means a difference in the "perception of faith and values".[1] Co-existing systems are perceived as differing in certain principles or values held as fundamental by parties involved in the difference, or even conflict. This is the case with the pluralistic religious society, such as exists in the modern western world. For example, among Jews and Christians there are certain shared principles and values but also many beliefs and values that both groups view as fundamental but which are nonetheless divergent or conflicting. The agreements in religious pluralism allow dialogue to take place and are, in fact, the basis for the ecumenical movement; but the differences are the chief obstacle to Christian unity in the West.

Here I have certainly drawn from more than one ecclesial tradition, but I have not been concerned as such with the major and real differences within the Christian tradition. I would hope, as a by-product of this effort, that Christian groups might find a different basis for their dialogic encounter that would facilitate co-operation and hasten the day of fuller unity.

3. Cultural pluralism.

What I have chosen to call "socio-cultural pluralism" is a further step along the line of separation of values. Not only do different religious traditions have value sets, but the major institutions of society now also propose their own value systems. This has been the level of my interest here, and the fact that I have attempted to support with empirical evidence. Further I have attempted to assess its importance and position in order to apply it to a theology of the Church. A rounded ecclesiology correlated with "socio-cultural pluralism" seems to me a necessity for our times.

It is important to indicate, in concluding this monograph, that the universality of revelation cannot be encapsulated in a single formula, like a creed, or even in a conditioned formulation, such as a theological system. Thus, "a multi-form Church in a pluralistic society" doesn't exhaust the nature of the Church, not even for our times. Rather universality is a mark of revelation and of the Church itself. The Church is not <u>simpliciter</u> one, in some kind of limited expression. One-ness must be balanced by and be in tension with universality. Thus the ecclesial expression, its concrete existence, must reflect the experience of universality, if the Church is to be a sign and a witness to the fulness of her responsiblity.

A multi-form Church is reaching toward this universality, without exhausting it or as yet achieving it. Yet in this very action of movement, of journey, of pilgrimage, the Church is "on the way" to the future. This multi-form Church is an open Church, a Church receptive of and accepting the future.

Nevertheless the Church open to the future is also an historical Church, and a Church conscious of her own history. We have seen, briefly, that the Church as reflected in the New Testament took several forms; and while we cannot return to those specific forms in a literal way, historical consciousness makes us acutely aware of the openness of the early Christian community. It is the theological perception behind this openness and its relationship to the orienting Christian communal experience that is the basis for the norms that we have been developing here. Even in a very different socio-cultural setting, we must remain in contact with the original revelation.

We have seen that today the Church does take on many forms simultaneously because of the nature of contemporary social institutions which are differentiated, diversified and outside the justifying "sacred canopy". This multi-form Church is certainly an Incarnational Church, because it is conditioned by the world; yet it must be careful to avoid compromise with the world. It is this same multiform Church as prophetic, charismatic, that struggles against the inevitable temptation to compromise. Yet it is precisely as incarnationally involved in the many institutions of a pluralistic society that the Church is the instrument to bring each of these institutions to fulness in its own way and as its own secular social area.

This is how the Church can now be co-creative of its own shape and destiny, for this is the opportunity for the Church to continue its mission in and to the world. The Church cannot and does not subsist in one form; this would seem to be either blind ethnocentrism or cultural arrogance. Rather the Church, in many forms, enters worldly institutions in response to the mission it has from Jesus, but conscious of the many directions and levels this response will move in. This is, as well, the way toward a solution of forms and structures in the Church; there is not a conflict among Christians who choose different forms, but divergence and diversity for the good of the whole Church and the accomplishment of its mission.

The Church as servant needs to become multiform because of society and society's members. Multiformity is necessary in our society with its great diversity and separation, in value systems, life-styles and self-justifying institutions. At the same time, people are no longer satisfied with one form of Church, or with monolithic unity. As human life itself becomes an infinite-possibility thing, so also the Church must provide service (and solace) in every area of this multiple universe.

We see then how the Church is both sign and instrument of salvation, of freedom, of fulness in Christ.[2] The Church is God's instrument in every arena; it is to be co-extensive with humanity in every institution and culture. At the same time

it is the sign of Incarnational unity, of that
complex one-ness that reflects and makes available
the liberating work of God. For it is not individuals
who are saved, one by one; it is mankind and men
and women in all their human institutions.

And so the Church, sign and instrument must
be present and available in all these institutions,
bringing them to salvation, to liberation, to that
fulness which God will give in his own Kingdom
of love, of justice, of peace.

REFERENCES

1. Pinto de Oliveira, Carlos-Josaphat, "The Church, Orthodoxy and a Pluralist Society", in Schillebeeckx, Edward (ed.) *Dogma* *and* *Pluralism*, *Concilium*, Vol. 51. New York: Herder & Herder, 1970. p. 96.

2. Cf. *Lumen* *Gentium*. Dogmatic Constitution on the Church, Vatican Council II. Chapter 1, 1.